child development
a primer

child development
a primer

Ingrid Crowther

Athabasca University

THOMSON

NELSON

Australia   Canada   Mexico   Singapore   Spain   United Kingdom   United States

THOMSON

NELSON

Child Development: A Primer
by Ingrid Crowther

Associate Vice President, Editorial Director:
Evelyn Veitch

Publisher:
Joanna Cotton

Marketing Manager:
Rosalind Wright

Senior Developmental Editor:
Lesley Mann

Photos:
Ingrid Crowther

Production Editors:
Carrie McGregor/Anne Macdonald

Copy Editor:
June Trusty

Proofreader:
Rohini Herbert

Indexer:
Belle Wong

Senior Production Coordinator:
Hedy Sellers

Design Director:
Ken Phipps

Interior Design:
Gail Ferreira
Ng-A-Kien

Cover Design:
Liz Harasymczuk

Cover Images:
Ingrid Crowther

Compositor:
Interactive Composition Corporation

Printer:
Transcontinental

Library and Archives Canada Cataloguing in Publication Data

Crowther, Ingrid, 1944-
    Child development : a primer/ Ingrid Crowther.

ISBN 0-17-641565-3

    1. Child development—Textbooks. I. Title.

HQ767.9.C76 2005   305.231
C2005-901979-4

Brief Contents

Contents

Preface

WHY WAS THIS BOOK WRITTEN?

The primary purpose of *Child Development: A Primer* is to give the reader an overview of the growth and development of children. Designed as a quick reference tool for parents, caregivers, and educators, it supports other learning activities, such as:

- Observing children.
- Identifying ages and stages of children.
- Guiding the selection of developmentally appropriate materials.
- Planning developmentally appropriate learning experiences.
- Organizing the learning environment to reflect and enhance the emergent skills of children.

ORGANIZATION OF THE BOOK

Child Development: A Primer is organized to maximize the reader's ability to find information expediently. Its 13 chapters are organized by section:

- Prologue: Prenatal Development
- Section 1: Infancy—Birth to Eighteen Months (Chapters 1 to 5)
- Section 2: The Toddler Years—Eighteen Months to Three Years (Chapters 6 and 7)
- Section 3: The Preschool Years—Three to Five (Chapters 8 to 10)
- Section 4: The Early School Years—Six to Eight (Chapters 11 and 12)
- Section 5: The Preteen Years—Nine to Twelve (Chapter 13)

The wealth of information in each chapter is presented in brief paragraphs, bulleted lists, and tables, and organized by category (e.g., "Physical Description" and "Cognitive Development"). Categories are repeated in basically the same order in each chapter to facilitate easy retrieval of information.

The organization of each chapter follows the changing pattern of development of children. As skills and abilities emerge, they are added to each chapter. Similarly, as skills become so refined that further changes are too small to be addressed, they are dropped from the discussion.

FEATURES OF THE BOOK

Child Development: A Primer includes several distinctive features to help the reader identify key information quickly and efficiently, including the following:

- Introductions to each section and chapter that highlight key developments for the particular age group
- Developmental Alerts throughout the book, in both the body of the text and as a column in many of the tables
- Discussion of cultural differences as appropriate
- Numerous photographs to illustrate the written text
- Diagrams and figures where appropriate

- Key terms to help readers understand new vocabulary (these are boldfaced in the text, presented in the margin with definitions, and consolidated in a glossary at the back of the book)
- Observation charts for specific age groups: These charts are cumulative, and many can be used with minor revisions for subsequent age groups; as new skills and behaviours emerge, new charts are added. Blank versions of these observation charts can be downloaded for your use from Nelson's Resource Centre for Early Childhood Education at www.ece.nelson.com.
- Appendixes providing more detailed information, including:
  - Appendix A: Developmental Milestones (combines developmental milestone charts and illustrative photographs for an informative look at both developmental areas, such as grasping and object permanence, and curricular areas, such as block play and sand play)
  - Appendix B: Theoretical Overview of Psychosocial and Cognitive Development (key aspects of the theories of Erik Erikson and Jean Piaget are summarized in this appendix)

UNDERLYING ASSUMPTIONS

The basic assumptions that underlie the information presented in this text relate to the following:

1. **Universality of development:** Most children progress through the same stages of development, although the rates of development may differ from child to child and may be culturally enhanced or delayed. Information has been presented that:
   - Addresses average development.
   - Includes some known cultural or individual differences as examples.
   - Is frequently represented in age ranges.

   It is important to note that there are differences in growth patterns and that these differences may not be cause for concern. Some children may exceed or be behind the stated developmental norms.

   Note also that children who have been exposed to abuse (physical and emotional), who have been diagnosed with special needs, who suffer from chronic illness, or who live in poverty may not develop at recognized normal rates.

2. **Creative development:** This area is not usually defined as a skill development area, but it is the author's firm belief that all children's activities are creative. Creativity has therefore been covered in all developmental domains.

3. **Provision of primary needs (food, clothing, shelter, stimulation, and affection):** It is assumed that the developmental areas discussed are under conditions in which children's primary needs have all been met. Research has strongly indicated, however, that individuals whose primary needs have not been met may experience long-lasting difficulties in all domains [McCain, M., & Mustard, F. (1999). *Early years study: Final report.* Toronto, ON: Government of Ontario, Publications Ontario; Begley, S. (1997). How to build a baby's brain. *Newsweek, 28,* 28–32].

ABOUT THE PHOTOGRAPHS

The numerous photographs in this book were all taken by the author in child-care centres and schools in five Canadian provinces and two territories, from the far North, in such places as Iqaluit and Whitehorse, to the urban southern centres of

Vancouver and Toronto. Through interaction with the many children in these photos and with their families, the author has been able to provide a much more precise and complete picture of child growth and development in the early years.

AUTHOR'S ACKNOWLEDGMENTS

I would like to acknowledge the help and assistance of all of the children whose photos you see in this text and of their families. I would also like to express my sincere appreciation to my colleagues for their reviews of and comments on the book proposal and manuscript. Their input has been most helpful in the development of this text. As well as some who wish to remain anonymous, these reviewers include:

Carol Anderson, Durham College

Diane Bergeron, George Brown College

Chris Cadieux, Fanshawe College

Velma Doran, Sheridan College

Patricia McClelland, Northern Lights College

Marian Pickton, North Island College

Lorraine Purgret, Centennial College

I would also like to thank June Trusty for her dedicated copyediting, as well as Nelson staff members Joanna Cotton, publisher, Social Sciences and Humanities; Alwynn Pinard and Lesley Mann, developmental editors; Carrie McGregor and Anne Macdonald, production editors; Angela Cluer, director, Media Development; Rosalind Wright, marketing manager; and Gail Ferreira Ng-A-Kien, interior designer.

ABOUT THE AUTHOR

Ingrid Crowther has earned her Doctor of Education in Early Childhood and the Middle Years. Her background includes teaching in early childhood, elementary school, university, and college programs. She has taught in England and in various provinces and territories across Canada.

Dr. Crowther has published articles in a variety of journals and has completed four additional textbooks: the first Canadian edition of *Infants and Toddlers: Curriculum and Teaching; Creating Effective Learning Environments* (also adapted for the American market and translated into German); *Introduction to Early Childhood: A Canadian Perspective;* and *Safe and Healthy Children's Environments.*

An adjunct professor at Athabasca University, Dr. Crowther has worked on several human services projects funded by Human Resources and Skills Development Canada and sponsored by Athabasca University: the Effective Practices project, the Pan Canadian Pathways project, and currently the Gateways project. An exhibition of her photographs of children was presented by the Yukon Art Society Gallery in Whitehorse in September 2005.

Prologue: Prenatal Development

"I can still remember the first time I felt my child kick. At first I thought I was imagining things but then, with the next kick, I knew that I was feeling my baby's movements. Suddenly, from being proud to be pregnant, I felt an overwhelming sense of love. It was my first physical link to my unborn child."

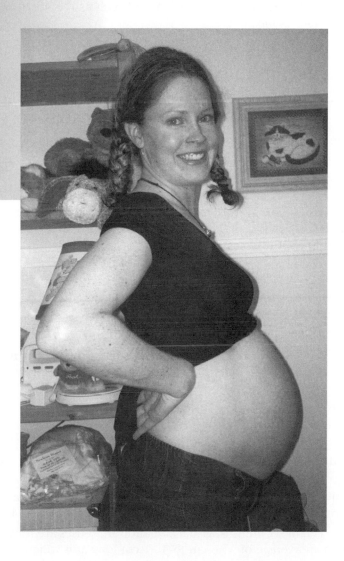

PERIODS OF PRENATAL DEVELOPMENT

Conception

- Penetration of the sperm into the ovum

Germinal Stage (Conception and Week 1)

- Rapid cell division begins—20 to 30 cells formed within three days.
- The cluster of cells moves toward the uterus.
- The embryoblast, a large cluster of cells, forms (develops into the placenta and other structures to support and nourish the developing embryo).
- Within four to five days, the embryo attaches itself to the uterine wall.
- Cell differentiation begins.

Embryonic Stage (Week 2 to Week 9)

- All major body structures begin to form, such as the heart, lungs, liver, brain, ovaries, and testes.
- Some organs start to function, such as the heart and the liver; blood production starts.
- Jaws, tooth buds, mouth, nose, and buds for arms and legs start to form.
- Neural tube forms at the end of the fourth week.
- During the second month, the growth rate is an average of 0.085 cm per day.
- In the fifth week, the cornea and lenses of the eyes develop; the eyes are shut.
- By the seventh week, the ears are formed, and a rudimentary skeleton is present.
- By the end of seventh week, development of the upper arms has begun, followed by development of the forearms, hands, and fingers; leg development follows a similar pattern.
- By the end of eight weeks, the embryo is an average of 3.8 cm in length and weighs about 2.8 grams.

Fetal Stage (Week 9 to Birth)

- In the third month, some reflexes develop, such as sucking and startle; movements of the arms and legs begin, such as kicking or making a fist; and swallowing and breathing motions are visible. The gender of the fetus can be detected by ultrasound.
- In the fourth month, motor actions become more refined; mother feels the first kick; the heartbeat can be heard with a stethoscope.
- By the end of the fourth month, the fetus looks human but cannot survive outside the womb.
- In the fifth and sixth months, eyelids, eyelashes, and eyebrows form: eyes are open: scalp hair develops: nails harden: skin thickens: and sweat glands are formed and operational. The fetus is covered with fine hair.
- By the end of six months, visual and auditory senses are fully functional. The fetus is an average of 35.6 cm to 38.1 cm long and weighs about 0.980 kg.
- In the final three months, growth and refinement of all body systems continue, to prepare the fetus for birth.
- After the seventh month, the fetus can survive outside the womb.

CRITICAL PERIODS OF PRENATAL DEVELOPMENT

There are several critical prenatal periods during which some environmental influences could cause both major and minor abnormalities. For example, the critical period for brain and central nervous system development is between conception and 16 weeks. Use of alcohol or exposure to radiation during this time could cause severe damage to the developing brain.

PROMOTING OPTIMAL PRENATAL DEVELOPMENT

Maintaining the expectant mother's health—both physical and emotional—is the focus of good prenatal care and should include the following:

- Regular medical checkups
- Rest and relaxation
- Regular exercise
- Proper nutrition; appropriate weight gain
- Good emotional health
- Good physical health
- Relative freedom from stress

Additional factors related to the mother that may influence optimal prenatal development include the following:

- Age of the mother—the early twenties to early thirties are optimal times for pregnancies
- Use of alcohol, tobacco, or certain drugs, including tranquilizers, antihistamines, and some over-the-counter medications
- Exposure to certain diseases, such as German measles
- Diseases or infections, such as syphilis, herpes, or acquired immune deficiency syndrome (AIDS)
- Exposure to pesticides or insecticides
- Drinking of products containing caffeine, including not only coffee but also some teas and soft drinks

Embryo and fetus vulnerable to damage from environmental influences, such as drugs, x-rays, infections

Embryo Development
- Major body structures develop
- Heart starts to beat
- Eyes, nose, ears form
- Arms and legs develop

Provide variances in activity—walking, resting
- Fetal behaviours (9–12 weeks)—kicking, thumb-sucking, mouth opening, and rehearsal breathing
- Fetal behaviour changes in response to mother's activity

HEAD
HAND
BODY
BABY

Provide appropriate nutrition and rest for optimal growth
- 30 days: An average of 5 mm long
- First trimester: By 5 weeks, an average of 12 mm long; by 9–12 weeks, an average of 7.6 cm long; fetal gender apparent
- Second trimester (13–24 weeks): By 5 months, an average of 25 cm long
- Third trimester (25–38 weeks): By end of period, an average of 50 cm long

13–24 weeks
Provide stimulation—talk to fetus, gently massage stomach, play soothing music
- By 5 months, fetal movements felt by mother
- By 24 weeks, neurons formed
  - Fetus reacts to sound
  - Eyes sensitive to light

25–38 weeks
Establish regular patterns of exercise, stimulation, and rest
- Sensory and behavioural capacities expand with brain development
- Antibodies transmitted to fetus
- Can survive early birth

INFANCY

Birth to Eighteen Months

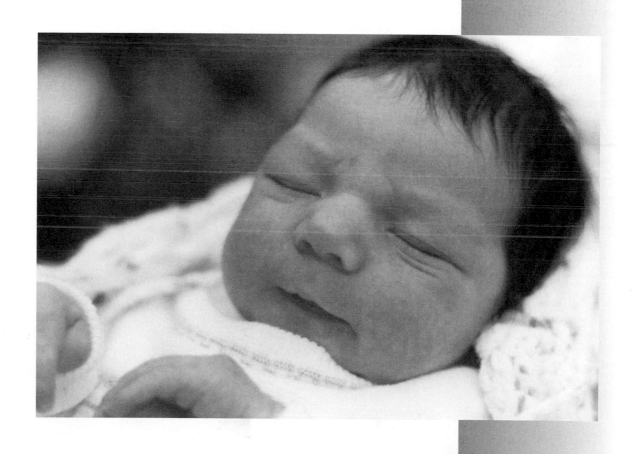

INTRODUCTION

The infant years are a time of remarkable growth and development. At no other time in their lives will infants grow and develop at such a tremendous rate. When infants are born, they come already equipped to ensure their survival. The infant recognizes the voices of the parents and turns toward them for comfort and fulfillment of needs. Many of the reflexes, such as sucking, help to ensure the infant's survival, guaranteeing that primary needs are met. These reflexes are either refined, such as the sucking reflex, or disappear as the infant grows and matures, such as the grasping reflex (this reflex becomes voluntary).

The infant's physical development also occurs in an ordered sequence according to need. Head and neck muscles develop first, enabling the infant to raise his or her head to prevent choking and also to turn the head to observe what is happening in the immediate vicinity. Muscle development continues as the infant's needs increase, and strength is gradually gained from head to foot and from the trunk outward.

These muscle developments are supported by spurts of brain growth—the brain rapidly develops neural connections, resulting in increases of brain size. These spurts correspond with the infant's activity at the time (see Table A). Increased neural activity can be measured by an electroencephalogram, or EEG, a test to detect the electrical activity of the brain (McCain & Mustard, 1999; Berk, 2002). Brain growth and increased neural connections help the infant to gain greater skills and abilities in all areas of development.

TABLE A	Spurts of Brain Growth in Infancy
APPROXIMATE AGE	**DESCRIPTION**
3 to 4 months	Infants reach for objects, grasp and manipulate them
10 months	Infants start to become more mobile, crawling and looking for hidden objects (object permanence)
12 months	Infants start to walk and become involved in active choices of what they wish to play with
1½ to 2 years	Language develops

During the first 1½ years, the infant learns to walk, starts to talk, develops a strong reciprocal relationship with caregivers, refines eye–hand coordination to effectively manipulate objects, learns to interact through vocalizations and body language, and actively explores the environment. Although infant development occurs along a developmental continuum, the rate and timing of individual development may vary.

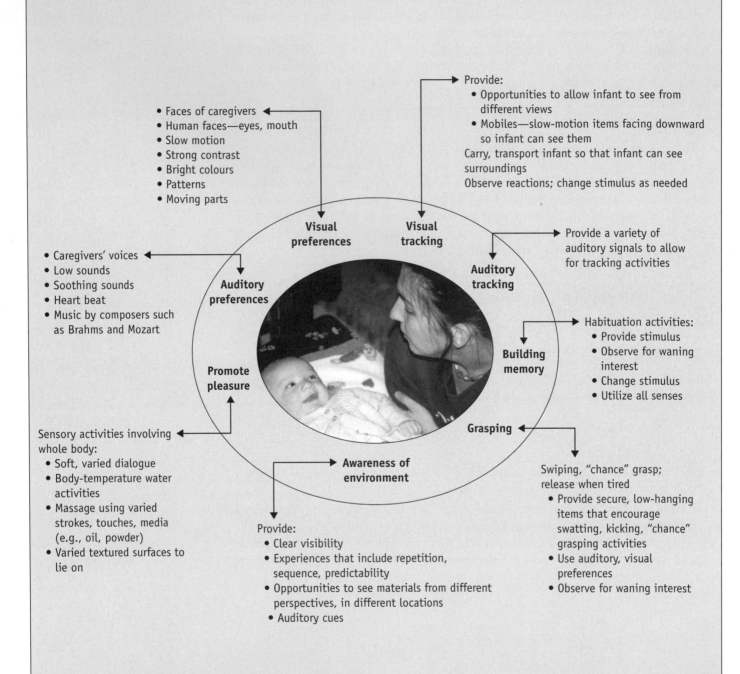

- Faces of caregivers
- Human faces—eyes, mouth
- Slow motion
- Strong contrast
- Bright colours
- Patterns
- Moving parts

Provide:
- Opportunities to allow infant to see from different views
- Mobiles—slow-motion items facing downward so infant can see them

Carry, transport infant so that infant can see surroundings
Observe reactions; change stimulus as needed

Visual preferences

Visual tracking

Provide a variety of auditory signals to allow for tracking activities

- Caregivers' voices
- Low sounds
- Soothing sounds
- Heart beat
- Music by composers such as Brahms and Mozart

Auditory preferences

Auditory tracking

Habituation activities:
- Provide stimulus
- Observe for waning interest
- Change stimulus
- Utilize all senses

Building memory

Promote pleasure

Grasping

Sensory activities involving whole body:
- Soft, varied dialogue
- Body-temperature water activities
- Massage using varied strokes, touches, media (e.g., oil, powder)
- Varied textured surfaces to lie on

Awareness of environment

Swiping, "chance" grasp; release when tired
- Provide secure, low-hanging items that encourage swatting, kicking, "chance" grasping activities
- Use auditory, visual preferences
- Observe for waning interest

Provide:
- Clear visibility
- Experiences that include repetition, sequence, predictability
- Opportunities to see materials from different perspectives, in different locations
- Auditory cues

CHAPTER 1

The Newborn—Birth to One Month

"For the first time you felt air on your skin and you moved your arms and legs in the air instead of water. There were strange noises. But in the middle of all other sounds was your mother's voice, one you already knew. You could see colours and lights and the curve and shine of things and the shape of people's faces smiling at you. They moved toward you and away from you. They were often blurry and fuzzy, like faces seen through frosted glass or in a mist" (Kitzinger & Nilsson, 1990, pp. 59–60).

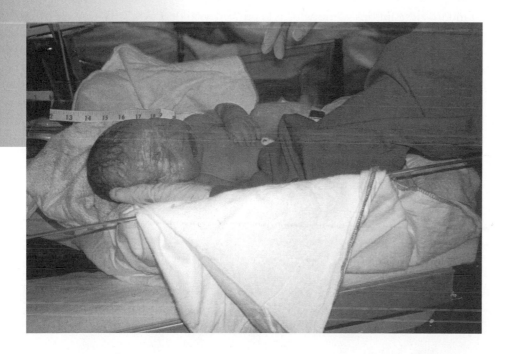

INTRODUCTION

Newborns come into the world already equipped with many skills to ensure their survival. They are born recognizing their primary caregivers' voices and the smell of their mothers and have the bodily systems ready to assume the responsibility of sustaining the new life. However, newborns cannot function independently—they are completely dependent on their caregivers to provide for their every need.

The newborn's behaviours are reflexive and are geared toward protection and sustainment of life. For example, when a nipple is placed in an infant's mouth, an automatic reflex sucking action is initiated. During the first month, infants gradually gain some control over some of their motor activities. Motor development proceeds in an orderly fashion, moving from the head downward (**cephalocaudal**) and from the trunk outward (**proximodistal**).

Initial interactions with caregivers are concerned with fulfillment of the infant's needs. The infant cries when hungry or uncomfortable. Gradually, these signals become more differentiated, and more and more social interactions become established. With the appropriate care and stimulation, the infant will gradually become a more alert, more social, and more active participant in the world around.

PHYSICAL DESCRIPTION

Standard descriptions of newborns mention wrinkled skin, the unusual shape of the head, and the relatively pale skin colour. What these descriptions omit is the parents' joy and fascination with their newborn child. Most parents regard the infant's birth as a small miracle. As one mother exclaimed, "Oh, he is soooo perfect. Look at the perfect little hands. Look at the perfect toes. Every detail is there. Oh, I love the hair. It is so fine and fuzzy. And look at that adorable stubby nose. It's just like his father's."

Infants are, indeed, a miracle. From the start they captivate the adults around them. This automatically ensures that the infant receives the attention and care needed. In one parent's words, "Who could not love such a small bundle of joy?"

cephalocaudal
motor development progression from the head downward to the legs and feet

proximodistal
motor development progression from the trunk outward to the arms and hands

PHOTO 1.1 "Who could not love such a small bundle of joy?"

TABLE 1.1 Physical Description—First Month

CHARACTERISTIC	AVERAGE	CHANGE	✳ DEVELOPMENTAL ALERT
Weight	2.5–4.5 kg; boys slightly heavier than girls	5–7% weight loss after birth; 0.14–0.17 kg weight gain per week	• Loss of weight • Not gaining weight Either could indicate insufficient nutritional intake
Size	45.7–55.9 cm in length	Grows about 2.54 cm over first month	• Lack of growth • Ensure that infant is getting enough nutrition
Body proportions	• High forehead • Head 31.7–36.8 cm in circumference • Head is ¼ of body length • Chest small, similar in size to head • Tongue appears large	• Gradual proportional changes in head size • Head circumference increases 1.9 cm over first month • Head size can be used to evaluate brain growth	Lack of gain in head size
Soft spots	Six soft spots (fontanels) at birth, but only two are visible: • Top of head (anterior) • Back of head (posterior)	Large spots may decrease in size, while smaller ones may increase in size	Care must be taken to protect the head
Respiration	• 30–50 breaths per minute • May be irregular	Increases during crying	Prolonged periods when breathing stops (apnea) may be a warning sign of sudden infant death syndrome (SIDS)
Temperature	35.6–37.2°C	Self-regulation of body temperature is irregular (could be caused by immature temperature-regulating mechanism)	• Hard to cool down or warm up infant • Increased body temperature is often the first indicator of illness, but either could indicate a lack of development of the temperature-regulating system

fontanels
soft spots on skull of infant

apnea
prolonged periods when breathing stops

SIDS
(sudden infant death syndrome) healthy infants die suddenly in their sleep for no apparent reason; danger peaks between 2 and 4 months, is over by one year of age

Table 1.1 continues on next page

TABLE 1.1 Physical Description—First Month

CHARACTERISTIC	AVERAGE	CHANGE	✳ DEVELOPMENTAL ALERT
Skin	Sensitive around mouth and hands	• Turns toward stimulus when stroked • Grasps items placed in hand • Heat escapes quickly from surface skin (infant has little body fat) • Does not shiver or perspire	• Does not turn toward stimulus and therefore may be harder to feed • Does not grasp items placed in hand

REFLEXES

A reflex is an automatic response to a stimulus. All healthy infants are born with reflexes, which serve a variety of purposes—ensuring survival, preparing the infant for the next stage of development, helping the infant to locate objects, and helping the infant to feed. Table 1.2 lists the common reflexes.

TABLE 1.2 Common Reflexes in Infants

REFLEX	DESCRIPTION	VALUE	AGE OF DISAPPEARANCE
Babinski	When sole of foot is stroked, toes fan and curl (**Babinski reflex**) (Photo 1.2)	Unknown	7–12 months
Blinking	Caused by a stimulant (e.g., air blowing into eyes or light shining in eyes, eyes close)	Protection of eyes	Permanent
Breathing	Inhale and exhale; present at birth	Survival—inhaling oxygen and exhaling carbon dioxide	Permanent
Crawling	When infant is placed face-down and mouth and nose are obstructed, head is raised and turned and arms and legs are extended and flexed	Survival—moving mouth and nose away from obstruction	Becomes more voluntary by 3–4 months
Gagging, coughing, sneezing	Air passages are cleared when blocked by mucus or other objects	Survival—clearing air passage to breathe	Permanent
Grasping	Automatically grasps finger or object placed in hand (Photo 1.3)	Preparation for various types of voluntary grasping and releasing of objects	3–4 months

Babinski reflex
when sole of foot is stroked, toes fan and curl

TABLE 1.2 **Common Reflexes in Infants** *(continued)*

REFLEX	DESCRIPTION	VALUE	AGE OF DISAPPEARANCE
Moro	When infant is startled by loud noise or jolted, arms are flung out, back is arched, and feet are extended; then limbs return toward body in embrace-like position (**Moro reflex**) (Photo 1.4)	Evidence of startling; might have helped infant cling to mother in evolutionary past	5–6 months
Rooting	Turns toward source of stimulation, such as stroking of cheek or corner of mouth (**rooting reflex**) (Photo 1.5)	Assists infant in finding nipple of bottle or breast	Becomes voluntary at 3 weeks
Stepping	When infant is held under the arms, feet touching a flat surface, stepping movements are made (Photo 1.6)	Prepares for voluntary walking	2–6 months
Sucking and swallowing	When nipple or another object is placed in infant's mouth, automatic sucking occurs; when nourishment is given, sucking is followed by swallowing	Helps infant to obtain nourishment	Permanent
Swimming	Kicking, paddling when placed facedown in water	Survival—learning to swim	4–6 months
Tonic neck	Head turned to side, one arm extended in front of eyes, opposite arm and leg bent at elbow and knee (Photo 1.7)	May prepare for voluntary reaching	4–7 months

Moro reflex
also known as the "startle response"; infant appears to be startled by an unexpected action or stimulant

rooting reflex
when corner of mouth or cheek is stroked, infant turns toward the source of stimulation

✳ **DEVELOPMENTAL ALERT**
The absence of any of these reflexes is potentially dangerous for the child.

PHYSICAL DEVELOPMENT

During the first month of life, many of the infant's physical behaviours are reflexive. These reflexive behaviours gradually become more refined, controlled, and purposeful. Some of these behaviours disappear completely.

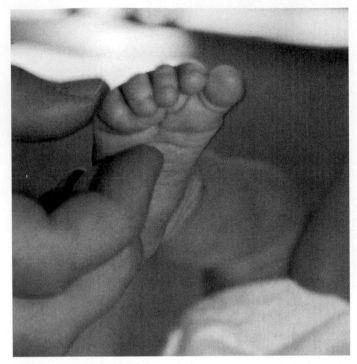

PHOTO 1.2 Babinski reflex

PHOTO 1.3 Grasping reflex

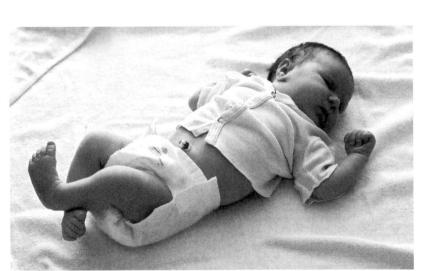

PHOTO 1.4 Moro (startle) reflex

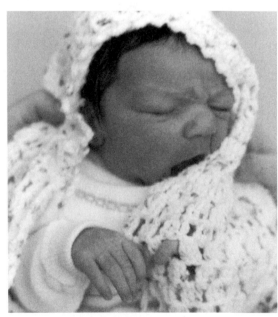

PHOTO 1.5 Rooting reflex

PHOTO 1.6 Stepping reflex

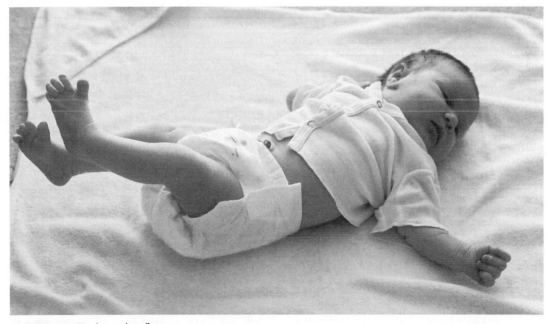

PHOTO 1.7 Tonic neck reflex

TABLE 1.3	**Physical Development—First Month**	
SKILL	**DESCRIPTION**	**✳ DEVELOPMENTAL ALERT**
Movement of head	• Moves from side to side while sitting with support or lying on back • Starts to lift head when on stomach—2 weeks to 2 months	• No movement of head • No movement of head toward a stimulus, such as a person entering the room (could indicate a hearing problem)
Body position	Back curled, arms and feet close to body (**fetal position**)	
Movement of arms, hands, and legs	• Very little control over movement • Hands and fingers put into mouth by chance • Grasps things reflexively when placed into hand • Releases items in hand when tired (lack of voluntary release) • Fingers curled into a fist	Lack of movement or very little movement

fetal position
back curled, arms and feet close to body

BEHAVIOURAL STATES

Infants establish a pattern of wakefulness and sleep shortly after they are born. These patterns are referred to as "behavioural states." This pattern soon becomes organized into predictable, individualized times of sleep and wakefulness. "Behavioral states are organized and cyclical—they appear in a predictable order, not at random" (Schickedanz et al., 2001, p. 103). A newborn tends to sleep about two-thirds of the time.

The periods of sleep and wakefulness become longer, eventually leading to the infant sleeping through the night. "[N]ewborns sleep as much in the day as at night, but within a few weeks, daytime sleep begins to drop and we see signs of day/night sleep rhythms (called 'circadian rhythms')—at least among infants in Western countries, where regular sleep/wake cycles are more highly valued. Babies at this age begin to string together two or three two-hour cycles without coming to full wakefulness, at which point we say that the baby can 'sleep through the night'" (Bee, 2000, p. 90).

Sleep and wakefulness patterns begin to be established during the first week and gradually change with time. Time spent sleeping in the first month is as follows (Bee, 2000, p. 91):

• Week 1: 8½ hours of sleep during the night and 8 hours of sleep during the day

• End of the first month: 8½ hours sleep during the night and 7½ hours of sleep during the day

Infants exhibit a variety of behavioural states during times of both sleep and wakefulness. These types are identified in Table 1.4.

TABLE 1.4	Sleep and Wakefulness Behavioural States—First Month	
STATE	**CHARACTERISTIC**	**SIGNIFICANCE**
Regular sleep	Little movement of body, eyes closed, regular breathing (36 breaths per minute), no response to mild stimulation but may startle to some stimulation (e.g., loud noises or a sudden, strong movement of the infant or its crib)	Continues to sleep with normal activity in the environment and if picked up
Irregular sleep	Increased movement of body (e.g., small twitches); facial expressions such as smiles and frowns; closed eyes with movement of eyeballs; irregular rhythm of breathing (up to 48 breaths per minute)	• More easily aroused by unusual stimuli • May wake when picked up
Periodic sleep	Between regular and irregular sleep, muscle movements and rapid breathing; periods of movement followed by short, quiet, calm periods	Starts to establish longer sleep patterns
Drowsiness	Some motor movement (less than during irregular sleep); eyes unfocused, open and close, regular breathing pattern; occasional high-pitched squeals	Signals need for sleep
Quiet awake	Eyes open, body relaxed, no movement, regular breathing	Starts to establish quiet times
Active alert	• Eyes open, looks toward sounds, looks around at things within visual range; turns head toward both visual and auditory stimuli; moves arms, legs, hands, and rest of body; alternates between periods of motor activity and relaxation • Body movements may be in response to stimuli such as talking to and touching infant; may use a variety of sounds such as moans and grunts	Signals that infant is alert and ready to interact
Crying, fussing	High motor activity (thrashing and twisting of body, flailing limbs, kicking); eyes may be open or partially shut; tears may appear; facial grimaces; fast, irregular breathing; whimpering, crying	Signals distress, intensity increases if not responded to (critical to respond to infant's need immediately)

Definite cultural variations can be observed in relation to infant sleep patterns. In North American cultures, children often have their own rooms with their own cribs and are expected to sleep in them, especially at night. In some other cultures, infants often sleep in a bassinet in the parents' room to facilitate instant attention during the night. Another common practice in some cultures is co-sleeping—the mother sleeps with the infant. One extensive research study revealed that 64 percent of parents in the 199 societies studied practised co-sleeping (Schickedanz et al., 2001).

Cultural variations have also been noted in attitudes toward crying and how long or how often an infant is carried, and a possible relationship has been established between these two practices. North American cultures seem to expect and accept a certain amount of crying as normal infant behaviour. Infants in such cultures as southern Mexico and Zambia who are often carried, however, have been reported to cry significantly less. "Parents can increase the carrying of their infants, and decrease their crying, by using an infant carrier. For very young infants, these carriers are designed as pouch-like sacs that the parent straps onto the front of his or her own body. An advantage of these devices is that the parent's hands are free even while carrying the baby. Thus, the baby experiences the security and warmth of the parent's body and can be carried more, but the parent can also tend to necessary tasks" (Schickedanz et al., 2001, p.109).

BRAIN DEVELOPMENT

"When a baby comes into the world her brain is a jumble of neurons, all waiting to be woven into the intricate tapestry of the mind" (Begley, 1996, p. 56).

After birth, infants must have experiences to make connections among the neurons in order to learn to make sense of their lives. This starts at birth. Every touch, every sound, every taste experience, every smell, and everything the infant sees starts this process of making connections among the neurons. Table 1.5 provides an overview of brain growth and development in the first month of life.

TABLE 1.5	Brain Development—First Month	
DEVELOPMENT	IMPORTANCE	AGE
100 billion neurons and 50 trillion connections	Enable infant to recognize parents' voices, smell of mother's milk, and caregivers' faces, and establish bonding and attachment	Birth
1000 trillion synapses	Early experiences strengthen connections and form new connections	End of first month

PHOTO 1.8 Being touched and held are important for the infant's brain development.

Research has shown a strong connection between how securely infants are attached to primary caregivers and the infants' development. The development of the brain is dependent on infants feeling secure; having good nurturing, good nutrition, and appropriate stimulation; being touched and held; and being responded to immediately and sensitively.

Healthy brain development creates the foundation of all future growth and development. "The quality of early sensory stimulation influences the brain's ability to think and regulate body functions" (McCain & Mustard, 1999, pp. 25–26). Early negative experiences have the opposite effect. Such experiences as an infant being left to cry for long periods of time or erratic caregiving patterns often lead to insecurely attached infants. These infants can have long-lasting patterns of behaviour that may be difficult to overcome in later life.

SENSORY DEVELOPMENT

"We know that infants can see, hear, taste, smell, and react to touch. But exactly how developed are these senses at birth? How does learning affect them? And what sensory abilities are likely to unfold as the infant develops?" (Dworetzky, 1996, p. 138)

Tables 1.6 through 1.10 identify critical experiences for optimal infant development that should be provided by caregivers.

TABLE 1.6	Visual Development—First Month		
SKILL	**DEVELOPMENT**	**CRITICAL EXPERIENCE**	**✳ DEVELOPMENTAL ALERT**
Acuity	• Pupil changes with brightness • Recognizes mother's face (acuity) • Vision is 20/400 at birth • Focuses best on objects that are 17.8–20.3 cm away	Visual stimulation necessary to create connections in the brain; without this stimulation in the first 6 months, sight does not develop normally even if the eyes were perfect at birth	Pupil size remains constant
Binocular fixation	Looks at objects with both eyes at same time (binocular fixation); develops by 1 month	Visual stimulation activities	Does not look at objects with both eyes at same time
Contrast sensitivity	Needs high contrast and boldness of lines to see; vision blurry	Visual stimulation that provides high contrast	Lack of interest in visual stimulation
Visual accommodation	Focuses best when 17.8–20.3 cm away	Provide stimulation within appropriate distance	Does not seem to look at objects
Tracking	Moves head and eyes in a jerky/smooth pattern to follow moving object	Sharp lines and moving parts	No evidence of visual tracking
Preference	Prefers sharp patterns and strong contrasts; human faces; red over white	• Sharp distinctive parts • Expressive human faces • Black and white patterns	Seems to lack interest in visual stimulation

acuity
sharpness of the visual image, or sound discrimination

binocular fixation
ability to focus on one object with both eyes

TABLE 1.7 Auditory Development—First Month

SKILL	DEVELOPMENT	CRITICAL EXPERIENCE	✳ DEVELOPMENTAL ALERT
Ears	Auditory canals filled with fluid at birth; clears within 3 days		Does not respond to auditory stimuli
Acuity	Sound needs to be louder for infant to hear than for adult	• Hears language, music • Communicates with adults	Not responsive to changing auditory stimuli
Tracking	Looks toward sounds within 3 days of birth	Speak to infant or make soft sounds from various parts of a room	Does not turn toward sounds
Distinguishable sound qualities	Soft/loud; high/low, long/short; ascending/descending tones, two and three syllables, and different stress on words	• Use expressive voices with rising tones, higher pitch • Provide a variety of auditory experiences (e.g., music, various soft sounds, talking) • Critical to developing language and emotional bond	Does not seem to be interested in being talked to or in auditory stimulation
Preference	Low soothing sounds; soothing music such as Brahms and Mozart; human voices; mother's voice; higher pitch	Adults should stimulate infants with various auditory experiences (see above)	No reaction to auditory stimulation

TABLE 1.8 Tactile Development—First Month

SKILL	DEVELOPMENT	CRITICAL EXPERIENCE	✳ DEVELOPMENTAL ALERT
Touch sensitivity	• Sensitive to touch around mouth or cheek, nose, skin of forehead, soles of feet, and genitals • Sensitive to temperature changes, especially cold • Sensitive to pain	• Use touch to soothe, calm • Use touch as an expression of pleasure and love	• Resists being touched, pulls away, stiffens body, cries • Insensitive to pain

TABLE 1.9 Development of Taste—First Month

SKILL	DEVELOPMENT	CRITICAL EXPERIENCE	✳ DEVELOPMENTAL ALERT
Preference	• Distinguishes sweet, sour, bitter, and salty • Recognizes mother's milk • Prefers sweet tastes; sucks longer and faster	Sweet tastes soothe infant and may act as a pain reliever	Lack of sucking or refusal to eat

TABLE 1.9	Development of Taste—First Month *(continued)*		
SKILL	**DEVELOPMENT**	**CRITICAL EXPERIENCE**	✳ **DEVELOPMENTAL ALERT**
Dislike	Salty, sour, and bitter tastes—will grimace, turn head away	Avoid providing tastes that infant dislikes	

TABLE 1.10	Development of Smell—First Month		
SKILL	**DEVELOPMENT**	**CRITICAL EXPERIENCE**	✳ **DEVELOPMENTAL ALERT**
Smell discrimination	• Recognizes mother's smell on first day • Has adult sense of smell • Turns away, grimaces, or cries in reaction to unpleasant smells	• Ensure that infant's room is well aired • Avoid exposure to unpleasant smells	No response to unpleasant smells

COGNITIVE DEVELOPMENT

Newborns come equipped with some cognitive skills, which become refined over the first month of life. Infants:

- Recognize primary caregivers' voices, the mother's heartbeat, and the mother's smell.
- Develop a sense of expectancy, evidenced by the infant looking toward a sound or a voice.
- Increasingly recognize and remember what is seen, heard, and touched (for example, Christopher at three weeks old would look at the faces on the mobile placed in visual range above his head. The faces, placed facedown so the infant could clearly see them, were interchanged periodically. He would move his eyes from one mobile face to another. When he found the one he was looking for, he would stop and gaze at it more intently).
- Respond to stimulation—wave and kick arms to indicate enjoyment, or may startle or cry at unexpected sounds or situations.
- Begin to show interest in what goes on around them by increasing eye contact, increasing sucking, and staring at the source of the stimulation.

COMMUNICATION

Newborns communicate through crying and through body activity. Interaction with newborns is critical to the development of communication skills and related social skills. They need to hear language and see facial expressions and body language to form the needed connections in the brain.

"At first, neurons in the auditory cortex are like labourers to whom jobs have not yet been assigned. But as a newborn hears, say, the pattern of English, a different cluster of neurons in the auditory cortex is recruited to respond to each phoneme" (Begley, 1997, p. 30).

Communication involves more than just talking to the newborn—facial expressions, intonation patterns, body language, listening, and turn-taking are also involved. Table 1.11 identifies some of the communication skills of newborns.

TABLE 1.11	Communication—First Month	
TYPE	DESCRIPTION	✴ DEVELOPMENTAL ALERT
Differential crying	• Nature and intensity of cry alerts caregivers to infant's need (e.g., indicates hunger, pain, discomfort, need for comforting, thirst, frustration, boredom, illness) • Ranges from whimper to intense cry of frustration	• Hard to comfort • Continual crying may signal illness or central nervous system distress
Variety of noises	Gurgles, throaty sounds; may start **cooing** at end of month	Lack of emotional expression
Listening	• Turns head toward sound • Looks at person speaking • Waves arms and hands or kicks when spoken to or touched	No response when spoken to or touched
Body language	• Signals wish to stop communicating by turning head away, looking away, yawning, squirming, or becoming placid • When excited, may kick or wave arms around • Facial expressions indicate like or dislike	• Too placid • Rigid or turns away from contact • Not attentive to faces

cooing
strings of vowel sounds with different intonation patterns and of varying volume

TEMPERAMENT

"Another way babies differ is in their temperament. Babies vary in the way they react to new things, in their typical moods, in their rate of activity, in their preferences for social interactions or solitude, in the regularity of their daily rhythm, and in many other ways" (Bee, 2000, pp. 97–98).

It is important to consider the newborn's individuality and to respond to it appropriately. Table 1.12 identifies various temperament types and some characteristics of each.

	TEMPERAMENT TYPES		
TABLE 1.12	**Temperament—First Month**		
FACTOR	**EASY CHILD**	**DIFFICULT CHILD**	**SLOW-TO-WARM-UP CHILD**
Activity level	• Regular patterns of eating, sleeping, wakefulness • During wakeful cycles, responds to interactions through facial expressions, eye contact, body movements • Shows interest through increased sucking • Is quiet to listen to voices, music, or certain sounds	• Irregular patterns of eating, sleeping, wakefulness • More time spent crying, or general fussiness • Hard to console • May turn away or stiffen body to resist cuddling • Higher-pitched crying • Hard time adjusting to new routines • Does not quiet to listen	• Sleeping and eating patterns more regular than difficult infant's • More passive in all activities; sucks less vigorously, less eye contact, less physical movement to show interest or excitement • Crying may be more of a whimper or low-pitched crying • May quiet to listen
Approach/ positive emotionally	Initiates contact through body movement, waving arms and hands, kicking, gurgling, crying, eye contact	Initiates activity through high-pitched crying, usually for personal needs	Rarely initiates contact, except for personal needs
Inhibition and anxiety	Usually not evident	In both familiar and new situations may: • Stiffen whole body when picked up • Turn head or eyes away • Fuss or cry	Seems indifferent when talked to or touched by new adults; may avoid eye contact, show no body movement, or be fussy
Negative emotionally/ irritability/anger	Usually positive facial expressions, body language, interactions with others	• Loud, high, piercing crying, fussiness • Arches away from contact	• Shows passive behaviours such as whimpering, ignoring others by turning away • Shows no excitement through body movement or facial expression
Effortful control/ task persistence	Maintains interactions by eye contact, vocalizations, body movements	Fussiness and crying seem persistent	Lack of initiation or maintenance of contact

PERSONAL/SOCIAL DEVELOPMENT

Research on life in the womb has led to some startling discoveries. The fetus responds by kicking to sudden loud noises, to high intensity of light, and to loud music. The fetus will relax when hearing the mother's voice or calming music and when the mother's abdomen is massaged. Prior to birth, enough vision has developed to allow the infant to see his mother and the sense of touch is highly developed. All of these aspects ensure that the infant and caregivers can establish a relationship shortly after birth (Hopson, 1998). Some of the characteristics of early interactions are described in Table 1.13.

TABLE 1.13	Personal/Social Development—First Month	
CHARACTERISTIC	**DESCRIPTION**	**✳ DEVELOPMENTAL ALERT**
Alertness	Caregiver talks to, smiles at, changes facial expressions, touches, holds, massages, or tickles infant while talking; infant may respond by watching eyes, vocalizing through gurgles or grunts, waving arms and hands, kicking	Lack of response to caregiver actions
Cuddling	Relaxes or calms when cuddled or held	Does not calm or relax when held
Trust	• Crying stops when infant sees parent or is picked up • Responds differently to different adults—relaxes when held by some adults, may tense or cry when held by others	Reaction is the same for all adult contacts
Turn-taking	By end of first month, will watch caregiver and then respond in a pattern of behaviour (e.g., caregiver tickles infant and infant waves hands and feet; cycle repeated)	No turn-taking evident

TOOLS FOR OBSERVING—BIRTH TO ONE MONTH

A variety of methods can be used to document the infant's progress, some of which can be started at birth and continued throughout the infant's development. These tools can be used to gain insight into the infant's interests or used to track possible medical problems or delays.

The following sample charts illustrate a simple way of recording the infant's various milestones, emotional development, and emerging and waning interests. Charts such as these should contain:

- Date on which an observation was made.
- Description of the development, activity, or behaviour.
- Any relevant additional comments.

Blank versions of these charts can be downloaded for your use from Nelson's Resource Centre for Early Childhood Education at www.ece.nelson.com.

SAMPLE 1

 Physical Development—Birth to 1 Month

Name: Jordaine

DEVELOPMENT	DATE	CHANGES/COMMENTS
Weight	Oct. 22	3.2 kg
	Oct. 23	3.0 kg, breast milk and supplement
	Oct. 26	3.05 kg breast milk only
Size	Oct. 22	52.4 cm long

Sample 2
Physical Development—Birth to 1 Month

Name: Jordaine

MOVEMENT	DATE	DESCRIPTION/COMMENTS
Head	Oct. 22	Right cheek stroked—turned head to right
Arms and legs	Oct. 22	Talked to infant and stroked body—moved arms and legs
Fingers	Oct. 22	• Fingers clenched in fist • When mother's finger placed in palm, grasped finger

Sample 3
Routines—Birth to 1 Month

Name: Jordaine

ROUTINE	DATE	TIME OR QUANTITY	NUMBER	COMMENTS
Sleep	Oct. 22	19 hours	5 cycles	
Feeding	Oct. 22	Breast feeding—first attempt was not successful, supplement given by nurse	3	Seemed to have trouble sucking; improved each time
Bowel movements	Oct. 22		2	During sleep

Sample 4
Interests—Birth to 1 Month (Enter interests as they are noticed)

Name: Jordaine

INTEREST	DATE	DESCRIPTION/COMMENTS
Tracking	Oct. 22	Someone entered room—followed movement with eyes
Music	Oct. 23	Cried, but calmed when Mozart was played

Sample 5
Communication—Birth to 1 Month

TYPE	DATE	DESCRIPTION/COMMENTS
Crying	Oct. 22	• Stopped when fed • Whimpered, soft crying—stopped when picked up
Vocalizations	Oct. 23	Gurgled and waved arms when tickled
Responses	Oct. 23	Watched eyes when talked to
Turn-taking		

FURTHER READING

Begley, S. (1996, February 10). Your child's brain. *Newsweek*, 54–58.

Begley, S. (1996, Spring/Summer). Special edition: Your child. *Newsweek*, 28–32.

Berk, L. (1999). *Infants, children, and adolescents* (3rd ed.). Needham Heights, MA: Allyn & Bacon.

Canadian Paediatric Society. (1994). *Little well beings: A handbook on health in family day care*. Ottawa, ON: Canadian Paediatric Society.

Dworetzky, J. (1996). *Introduction to child development* (6th ed.). St. Paul, MN: West Publishing Company.

Hopson, J. (1998, September/October). Fetal Psychology. *Psychology Today*, 44–49.

Pucket, M., & Black, J. (2001). *The young child development from prebirth through age eight* (3rd ed.). Upper Saddle River, NY: Merrill/Prentice Hall.

Schickedanz, J., Schickedanz, D., Forsyth, P., & Forsyth, G. (2001). *Understanding children and adolescents* (4th ed.). Needham Heights, MA: Allyn & Bacon.

Watson, L., Watson, M., Cam Wilson, L., & Crowther, I. (2000). *Infants and toddlers* (1st Cdn. ed.). Scarborough, ON: Nelson Thomson Learning.

REFERENCES

Bee, H. (2000). *The developing child* (9th ed.). Needham Heights, MA: Allyn & Bacon.

Begley, S. (1997). How to build a baby's brain. *Newsweek, 28*, 28–32.

Berk, L. (2002). *Infants and children* (4th ed.). Boston, MA: Allyn & Bacon.

Dworetzky, J. (1996). *Introduction to child development* (6th ed.). St. Paul, MN: West Publishing Company, 138.

Hopson, J. (1998, September/October). Fetal Psychology. *Psychology Today*, 44–49.

Kitzinger, S., & Nilsson, L. (1990). *Being born*. Ringwood, Victoria, Australia: Penguin Books, 59–60. This book is a wonderful photographic representation of the developing fetus through to birth. Explanations are provided from the fetus's viewpoint.

McCain, M., & Mustard, F. (1999). *Early years study: Final report*. Toronto, ON: Publications Ontario.

Schickedanz, J., Schickedanz, D., Forsyth, P., & Forsyth, G. (2001). *Understanding children and adolescents* (4th ed.). Needham Heights, MA: Allyn & Bacon.

GROSS EXPLORATION STAGE

During the first four months of life, infants are totally dependent on their caregivers to provide appropriate stimulation in all areas. Infants' actions become more refined as they learn to react appropriately to the stimulation provided. For example, swatting at items becomes refined to reaching for and accurately grasping an item within reach.

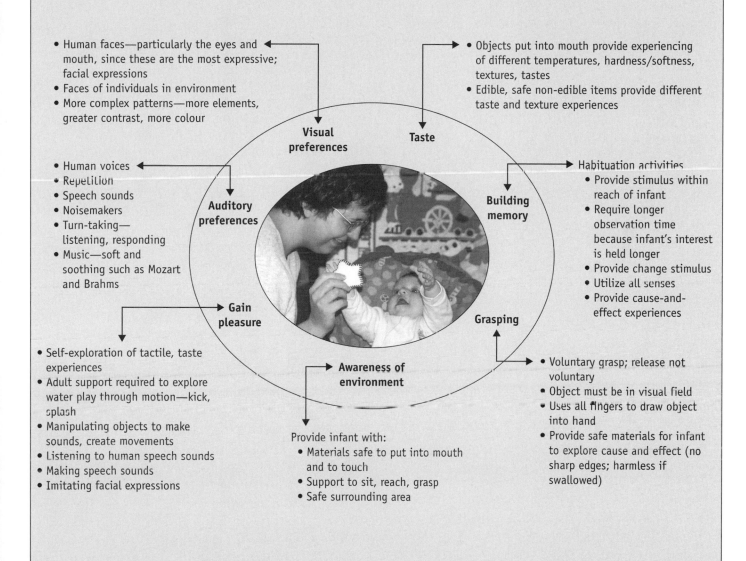

Visual preferences

- Human faces—particularly the eyes and mouth, since these are the most expressive; facial expressions
- Faces of individuals in environment
- More complex patterns—more elements, greater contrast, more colour

Taste

- Objects put into mouth provide experiencing of different temperatures, hardness/softness, textures, tastes
- Edible, safe non-edible items provide different taste and texture experiences

Auditory preferences

- Human voices
- Repetition
- Speech sounds
- Noisemakers
- Turn-taking—listening, responding
- Music—soft and soothing such as Mozart and Brahms

Building memory

Habituation activities
- Provide stimulus within reach of infant
- Require longer observation time because infant's interest is held longer
- Provide change stimulus
- Utilize all senses
- Provide cause-and-effect experiences

Gain pleasure

- Self-exploration of tactile, taste experiences
- Adult support required to explore water play through motion—kick, splash
- Manipulating objects to make sounds, create movements
- Listening to human speech sounds
- Making speech sounds
- Imitating facial expressions

Awareness of environment

Provide infant with:
- Materials safe to put into mouth and to touch
- Support to sit, reach, grasp
- Safe surrounding area

Grasping

- Voluntary grasp; release not voluntary
- Object must be in visual field
- Uses all fingers to draw object into hand
- Provide safe materials for infant to explore cause and effect (no sharp edges; harmless if swallowed)

CHAPTER 2

One to Four Months

"I thoroughly enjoyed my son's emergent personality. He was so eager to learn. He continually watched me and, as he grew older, imitated many sounds and gestures. I loved to coo at him and have him coo back with delight. I loved to watch his face light up when he saw me enter the room after a nap. I will always remember and treasure these moments of our personal times together" (mother of a three-month-old son).

INTRODUCTION

Infancy is a time of rapid change. Infants grow and expand their skills at a rapid rate, moving from total dependency to gradual independence as they become more mobile, learn to control their muscles, explore their world, and gradually learn to talk.

Infants develop rapidly during the first four months of life. Not only is there evidence of rapid physical growth, but also signs of social, emotional, cognitive, and language growth. Individual differences may be observed:

- Timing: Infants may develop skills more quickly or more slowly than their peers. This is dependent on maturation, stimulation, and individual abilities.
- Pacing: Some infants move through each growth phase more quickly or more slowly than others. Normative data imply that all infants have identical experiences, but experiences vary from situation to situation and from culture to culture.

Longer periods of alertness and more regular patterns of eating and sleeping develop during these first four months. Infants start to interact more socially with their caregivers, imitating sounds and gestures, smiling, and reacting with excitement to stimuli that they enjoy. These social interactions strengthen the attachment between the infants and the adults in their environment. These weeks in an infant's life are an enjoyable time for both infants and their caregivers.

It is important to provide stimulation for the infant at this time to encourage all types of development—physical, social, emotional, cognitive, and language. For example, holding an infant enhances the infant's ability to regulate his or her body temperature, provides a soothing activity for both infant and caregiver, and provides opportunities for social interaction and learning.

PHYSICAL DESCRIPTION

During these three months, growth proceeds rapidly. As infants gain weight and length, their body proportions also begin to change.

TABLE 2.1	Physical Description—1 to 4 Months		
CHARACTERISTIC	**AVERAGE**	**CHANGE**	**✳ DEVELOPMENTAL ALERT**
Weight	Average weight: 3.6–7.3 kg	• Average gain: 0.5–1 kg per month • Weight gain dependent on infant's temperament: Mellow, more laid-back infants burn fewer calories and therefore gain weight more quickly. Conversely, active infants burn more calories and therefore tend to be leaner	Lack of weight gain
Size	Average length: 50.8–68.6 cm	Average growth: 2.5 cm per month	Lack of increase in size

TABLE 2.1	Physical Description—1 to 4 Months *(continued)*		
CHARACTERISTIC	AVERAGE	CHANGE	✳ DEVELOPMENTAL ALERT
Body proportions	Increase in body fat gives the infant a more plump look	• Head and chest circumferences almost the same • Arms and legs same length, size, and shape, although legs may appear slightly bowed and feet are flat	Lack of increase in circumferences
Head Size		Head circumference increases in size by about 1.9 cm per month during first 2 months and about 1.6 cm during last 2 months	
Soft spots (fontanels)	Timing of closing varies	Posterior fontanel usually closes by second month; anterior fontanel closes to about 1.3 cm, the last soft spot to disappear (Dr. Greene, 2003)	A large anterior fontanel that does not close may be associated with some uncommon conditions
Respiration	30–40 breaths per minute	• Infant uses abdominal muscles to breathe • Breathing rate increases with activity or while crying	• Irregular breathing • Periods of not breathing at all
Temperature	From 8–9 weeks, can regulate own body temperature	Normal temperature: 35.7–37.5°C	

REFLEXES

Many of the infant's original reflexes become weakened during this time frame or disappear completely; for example, the tonic neck and stepping reflexes disappear and the grasp reflex weakens. Some survival reflexes, such as rooting and sucking, are well developed at this point, although the swallowing reflex is still developing. The infant still has some difficulty in using the tongue to move food to the back of the throat and consequently is still drooling. A new reflex, the Landau reflex, emerges between 3 and 10 months—when held in a facedown position, infants hold up their heads and extend their arms and legs (Boon, 2004). For more information on various reflexes, see Chapter 1.

✳DEVELOPMENTAL ALERT
If reflexes such as tonic neck, stepping, and weakening of the grasp have not disappeared by the fourth month, this may be indicative of possible medical conditions, such as cerebral palsy (Winzer, 1999).

PHYSICAL DEVELOPMENT

During this period, infants gradually gain control of their movements, which become refined and less jerky. They can visually explore the environment by turning their heads toward sounds, and can express themselves by waving their arms. Encouraging movement will help infants to strengthen their muscles.

TABLE 2.2	Physical Development—1 to 4 Months	
SKILL	**DESCRIPTION**	**✳ DEVELOPMENTAL ALERT**
Movement of head	• Head turns side to side • By fourth month, holds head up in line with body • Head and upper body raised when lying facedown (Photo 2.1) • By fourth month, head held steadily	Lack of these head movements
Body movement	• Early movements are large and jerky but become more refined • By fourth month, infant rolls from front to back and back to front; when rolling, infant leads with head, body follows (Photo 2.2) • When pulled to a sitting position, head lags and back is rounded • At end of period, sits with support and head is steady • Moves to music, singing, or chanting • Expresses excitement by kicking and flailing arms • Upper body movement prevalent	• Movements stay large and jerky • Infant very placid with little attempt to move, even with stimulation
Fine motor	• Uses entire hand to grasp (Photo 2.3) • Releases object when tired • Hands held in open or semi-open position • Hands clasped in front of face • Waves hands, wiggles fingers • Reaches for objects, but may not be successful at grasping in early stages • Eye-hand coordination—swats at items within reach, grasps by chance by about 2½ months • Thumb-sucking may start • By 2 months, can twist the wrist to look at objects from different perspectives • By the fourth month, starts to shake or wave held objects	Does not reach toward people or objects

SLEEP PATTERNS

Infant sleep patterns differ, but overall there are an increasing number and longer periods of wakefulness. By six weeks, infants start to sleep longer, from three to five hours, especially in the evenings. By three to four months, they develop regular sleep and wakefulness patterns, averaging from three to five hours of sleep during the day that may be grouped into several nap times. Infants will sleep from 10 to 12 hours at night, but may still need one or two feedings during this time.

BRAIN DEVELOPMENT

Brain development increases at a rapid rate during these first months. As the brain's neural connections develop, the infant starts to be able to make sense of the world. For example, when the infant reaches and grasps an object, connections are formed and then strengthened to develop eye–hand coordination and provide

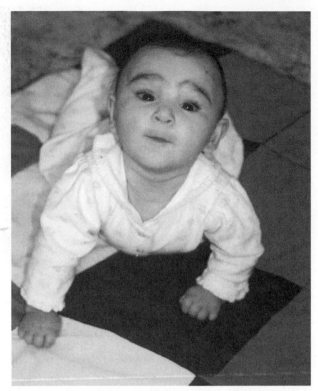

PHOTO 2.1 An infant will raise her head and upper body when lying facedown.

PHOTO 2.2 To roll, the infant leads with her head, followed by the rest of her body.

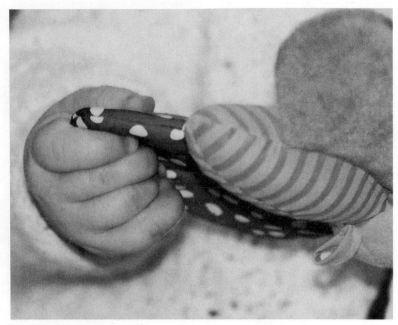

PHOTO 2.3 The infant uses her entire hand to grasp objects.

factual information about the object (e.g., size, colour, shape), and memories of these experiences are formed.

TABLE 2.3	Brain Development—1 to 4 Months	
CHARACTERISTIC	**IMPORTANCE**	**AGE**
Neural connections increase more than 20 times, to 1000 trillion	• Influences all learning • Through these connections, infants learn to make sense of what they see, hear, smell, taste, and touch • Early experiences continue to strengthen the connections and form new connections	By 3 months
Increased myelination	**Myelination** is a process that forms a sheath around nerve fibres. This sheath helps to speed up the rate of transmission of impulses (see Figure 2.1)	Continuous process after birth
Increased number of glial cells	**Glial cells** provide nutrients to the nerve cells, carry away waste products, and repair damage	Continuous process after birth

myelination
process by which a protective sheath is formed around nerve fibres; this sheath helps to speed up the rate of impulse transmission

glial cells
cells that provide nutrients to the nerve cells, carry away waste products, and repair damage

SENSORY DEVELOPMENT

The infant's visual acuity gradually improves, leading to increased ability to detect colour, pattern, and movement.

FIGURE 2.1 **Nerve Cell**

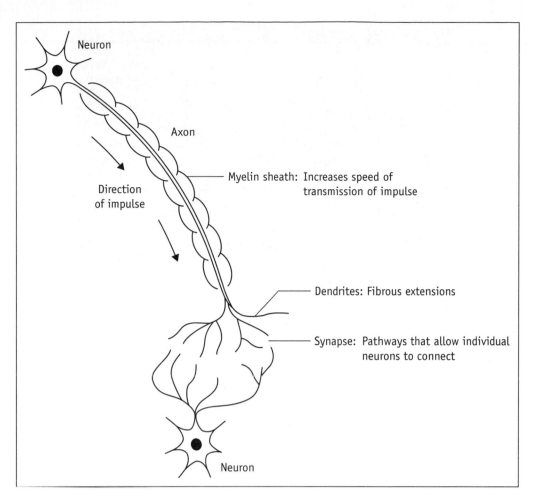

Neuron

Axon

Direction
of impulse

Myelin sheath: Increases speed of
transmission of impulse

Dendrites: Fibrous extensions

Synapse: Pathways that allow individual
neurons to connect

Neuron

TABLE 2.4   Visual Development—1 to 4 Months

CHARACTERISTIC	DEVELOPMENT	❋ DEVELOPMENTAL ALERT
Visual acuity	• **Contrast sensitivity:** By 3 months, the degree of contrast needed to detect patterns is similar to that needed by an adult • **Temporal resolution:** By 2 months, the ability to differentiate between a light that is flashing and a constant light is the same as an adult's • **Visual accommodation:** By 2–3 months, the ability to change the shape of the eye's lens to focus on objects at different distances is similar to an adult's • **Tracking:** By 8–10 weeks, smoother eye movements lead to the ability to target what to look at; to follow a moving object vertically and horizontally; and to continue to look in the direction of a disappearing object	• Inability to track • Ignores objects seen at a distance • Does not reach out for objects or individuals nearby
Preferences	Faces, complex patterns	Does not react to visual stimuli

contrast sensitivity
the degree of contrast that is needed for a pattern to be detected

temporal resolution
ability to differentiate between a light that is flashing and a constant light

visual accommodation
ability to change the shape of the eye's lens to focus on objects at different distances

tracking
visually following the movement of an object

TABLE 2.5 Auditory Development—1 to 4 Months

CHARACTERISTIC	DEVELOPMENT	✷ DEVELOPMENTAL ALERT
Location of sounds	Looks toward sounds	Does not turn toward sounds
Recognition of sounds	• Familiar voices • Familiar sounds • Familiar music, songs • At 4 months, infant is more attentive to spoken approval than to spoken disapproval	Does not seem to recognize familiar voices or sounds
Preference	• Familiar sounds, music, caregivers' voices • Low, soothing sounds • Cooing sounds	Shows no auditory preference

TABLE 2.6 Tactile Development—1 to 4 Months

CHARACTERISTIC	DEVELOPMENT	✷ DEVELOPMENTAL ALERT
Touch	• Has increased sensitivity, especially to temperature and pain • May start to develop tactile preferences (e.g., prefers the feeling of a particular surface or toy) • Begins to put objects into his or her mouth	Insensitive to tactile stimulation

EATING

An early milestone is reached when an infant begins to actively communicate the need for food by reaching for the mother's nipple. Also during this period, eating patterns become more regular and predictable. These patterns are influenced by food preferences developed by the infant in response to being given items such as sweetened water or apple juice, and by whether a demand-feeding or scheduled-feeding routine has been followed.

A variation in eating patterns also occurs when children are started on solid foods, when increased fussiness in anticipation of being fed can be observed. Although the amounts and times an infant eats will vary from infant to infant, the averages are as follows:

- Number of feedings for average-sized infant: Up to seven times per day
- Amount: 158–177 ml of food per day

- Danger of later obesity and anorexia is related to feeding on too rigid a schedule
- Insufficient feeding

TASTE/SMELL

During the first to fourth months, the infant:

- Gains increased ability to distinguish tastes, with resultant changes in preferences (e.g., prefers salty water to plain water by four months, and will nurse longer by one month if the mother has ingested vanilla).
- Will turn head away, grimace, or fuss in reaction to unpleasant smells.

❋ DEVELOPMENTAL ALERTS

- Lack of preferences
- Lack of reaction to strong smells or different taste experiences

COGNITIVE DEVELOPMENT

A number of changes in cognitive behaviours occur during the first fourth months. Infants' increasing ability to manipulate objects expands their awareness of the world around. The interplay between their fine motor, gross motor, visual, and auditory senses leads to increased cognitive development and to ever-greater exploration of their environment. By three to four months, infants:

- Start to hold and visually examine an object they are holding (see Photo 2.4).
- Hold an object in one hand and explore the object with the other hand.
- Repeat actions that they enjoy, such as holding and shaking a favourite toy.

As a result of the interplay of all of these factors, the infants' ability to increase their understanding of the world around them is demonstrated through their ability to:

- Distinguish an increasing number of colours.
- Demonstrate an awareness of size—may be frightened of something that is larger than they are.

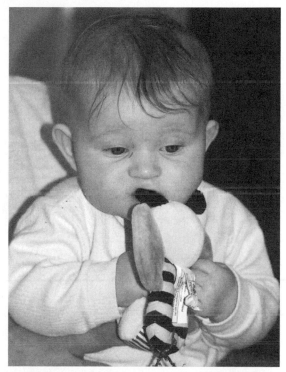

PHOTO 2.4 By three to four months, the infant starts to visually examine held objects.

PHOTO 2.5 The infant can make choices when an opportunity is presented.

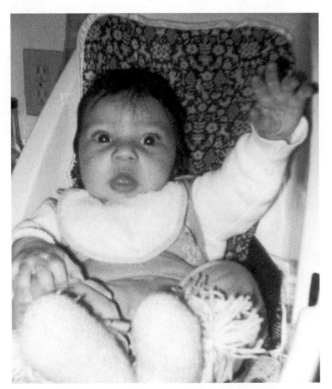

PHOTO 2.6 The infant can imitate gestures, such as waving.

- Recognize familiar objects, such as a feeding bottle.
- Recognize different shapes, such as a favourite toy held upside down.
- Actively make choices if the opportunity is provided (see Photo 2.5).
- Distinguish known faces from those of strangers.
- Imitate actions and gestures that have been seen previously, such as waving (see Photo 2.6).
- React differently to various sounds and voice tones—may frown at unfamiliar sounds or voices, may look anxious when hearing raised voices.
- Recognize favourite music and be soothed or excited—may relax when hearing a Brahms lullaby or become excited when hearing the caregiver sing a favourite nursery rhyme.

COMMUNICATION

Infants continue to build their repertoire of gestures, facial expressions, body language, listening, and turn-taking. A number of new milestones emerge during this one- to four-month period, as shown in Table 2.7.

TABLE 2.7 Communication—1 to 4 Months

TYPE	DESCRIPTION	✳ DEVELOPMENTAL ALERT
Cooing	• Combination of various vowel sounds, such as "eeee," "oooo" • Adds pitch, volume, and intonation patterns to coos, such as a long "oooo" sound with a high pitch variation, changes in volume, and ending in a higher pitch	Lack of cooing
Cry differential	May cry, stop and listen to see if there is a response, and start to cry again	• Continued crying • Hard to soothe
Communication maintenance	• Uses eye contact to continue communication • Listens, then responds • Reacts to voices, turning toward the sound and responding appropriately even when the speaker is out of visual range • Watches speaker and uses body language and facial expressions to communicate, such as smiles when smiled at or laughs when tickled	• No eye contact • No interactive communication
Imitation	Imitates coos, facial expressions, body language, and other communicative gestures	No imitation evident

TEMPERAMENT

Differences in patterns of behaviour established during the first month tend to persist through childhood. However, that does not imply that these characteristics remain fixed. Changes in temperament are shaped by the following:

- Experiences of the infant
- Patterns of interactions with caregivers
- Relationships with individuals around them

PERSONAL/SOCIAL DEVELOPMENT

The continued increasing abilities of the infant in the physical, language, and cognitive domains have a profound effect on the infant's interactions with others. During the first four months, the infant has gained skill in:

- Initiating and maintaining interactions, such as crying for attention, listening for a response, crying again, and then stopping the crying when a caregiver enters the room.
- Avoiding or ending interactions that are not satisfying by using a larger repertoire of skills, such as turning away, yawning, avoiding eye contact, quieting body movement, or starting to fuss.
- Reacting differently with various individuals, depending on the person's tone of voice.
- Responding with a wider range of response patterns, such as smiling or laughing appropriately to the stimulus provided, cooing, or squealing with enjoyment.
- Demonstrating enjoyment of activities such as being tickled or cuddled or bath time routines.

PLAY

solitary play
playing alone without interaction with others

TABLE 2.8	Play—1 to 4 Months
TYPE OF PLAY	**DESCRIPTION**
Solitary	Engages in **solitary play**: • Plays with own body parts—looks at them, waves arms, hands, fingers, feet • Keeps toys in motion by swatting or hitting them with hands or feet • Puts objects in mouth • Entertains self (e.g., by cooing, playing with crib toys; see Photo 2.7) • Shakes noisemakers repetitively and gurgles or laughs at the sounds made
Interactive	• Play with adults—enjoys interactive activities, such as peek-a-boo games, and being tickled, bounced, or rocked • Listens to singing games and expresses enjoyment by body movements, facial expressions, and/or vocalizations
Imitative	• Toward end of the period, imitates gestures (e.g., pats own head after someone has done this to him or her) • Imitates vocalizations—cooing, intonation patterns

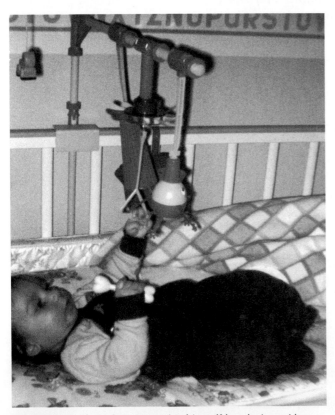

PHOTO 2.7 The infant entertains himself by playing with crib toys.

❋ **DEVELOPMENTAL ALERT**
Passive behaviour; does not engage in either solitary or interactive play

TOILETING

By the fourth month, infants usually have an average of two bowel movements per day.

❋ **DEVELOPMENTAL ALERT**
Excessive or no bowel movements

TOOLS FOR OBSERVING—ONE TO FOUR MONTHS

The following sample observation charts illustrate a simple way of recording the infant's various milestones, emotional development, and emerging and waning interests. Blank versions of these charts can be downloaded for your use from Nelson's Resource Centre for Early Childhood Education at www.ece.nelson.com.

Observation of the infant's skills at this stage will enable the caregiver to:

- Engage in relevant interactions.
- Provide appropriate choices for the infant.
- Ensure the health and safety of the infant.
- Provide appropriate materials and experiences.

SAMPLE 1
Gross Motor Skills—1 to 4 Months

Name: Christopher

SKILL	DATE	OBSERVATION
Lifted head	Oct. 29 Nov. 1	• Lifted head and upper body • Lifted head and body, turned head toward caregiver and smiled
Rolled over	Dec. 1	Saw his favourite toy out of reach; rolled over to it to grasp it
Sat	Oct. 30	Sat with support of large pillow; head straight

Possible Interpretations
1. Is looking for approval of his newfound ability because he lifted head and smiled. Reinforce his behaviour to indicate pride in his achievement.
2. Needs incentive to roll over. Place other favourite materials just out of reach to encourage this behaviour.
3. Provide opportunities to sit with support. Provide materials within reach when he is sitting so that he does not fall over when reaching for them.

SAMPLE 2
Fine Motor Skills—1 to 4 Months

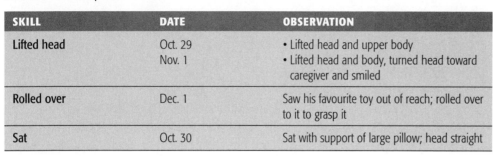

Name: Christopher

SKILLS	DATE	OBSERVATION
Grasping	Nov. 1 Nov. 2 Nov. 5	• Swatted at bells attached to a hanging mobile over his head; squealed every time the bells jingled • Shook hand with wristband with bells in it; smiled and laughed when he heard the sounds • Grasped soft cloth sound cube near him; brought it close to his face, stared at it, then put a corner of it into his mouth

Possible Interpretation
Christopher likes the added dimension of sound. Provide other items that have sound-making capabilities.

SAMPLE 3
Preferences

Observation of infant preferences can help in identifying the following:

- Interests
- Choices of play materials
- Most enjoyable play activities
- Length of attention span

- Preferred interactive activities
- Activities that should be avoided because the infant does not like or is frightened by the activity

Preferences—1 to 4 Months

Name: Melanie

LIKE	DISLIKE	DATE
• Fuzzy, bright pink bunny—grasped, shook, looked at, tried to put into mouth • Played with bunny until she dropped it, then continued to play with bunny when it was given back to her; this activity was repeated four additional times		Oct. 22
	Jazz music—father put on new Benny Goodman CD, Melanie startled and started to cry; cried until music was turned off	Oct. 23

Possible Interpretation

1. Melanie drops the toy when her hand is tired. She needs someone to give it back to her to encourage continued play.
2. Melanie is frightened by certain types of music. These types of music should be avoided.

SAMPLE 4

Language—1 to 4 Months

Name: Christopher   **Dates:** Oct. 1, 2, 3

LANGUAGE ACTIVITY	DESCRIPTION
Cooing	• Used all vowel sounds • Used low and high pitches with variation • Cooed when alone or playing with toys
Imitation	Imitated pitch and coos
Initiation	Initiated cooing sound, looked at caregiver, and waited for caregiver to repeat the sound; laughed and kicked feet when the sound was repeated

Possible Interpretations

Christopher enjoys the social interaction of dialogue. He has grasped turn-taking and how to continue communication. Additional opportunities to do so should be provided.

SAMPLE 5
Play—1 to 4 Months

Name: Melanie   **Dates:** Nov, 1, 2, 3

TYPE OF PLAY	DESCRIPTION
Solitary	• Played with her fingers and feet before going to sleep • Played with mobile toys held over her head when lying on the floor
Imitative	• Returned "bye-bye" wave • Imitated coos, intonation patterns • Imitated tongue movement
Interactive	• Rhyming games—"This Little Piggy" • Singing games—"Head and Shoulder," with caregiver doing the actions for the infant

Possible Interpretations
1. Melanie is at an age-appropriate level for her types of play.
2. She seems to enjoy musical and rhyming games, and so these activities could be expanded.

REFERENCES

Boon, R. (2004). *What are primitive reflexes?* Learning Discoveries Psychological Services. Retrieved October 11, 2004, from http://home.iprimus.com.au/rboon/NeurodevelopmentalTherapy.htm.

Dr. Greene. (2003). *Soft spots: Caring for the next generation.* Retrieved October 12, 2004, from www.drgreene.com/21_855.html.

Winzer, M. (1999). *Children with exceptionalities in Canadian classrooms.* Scarborough, ON: Prentice Hall Allyn & Bacon.

CHAPTER 3

Four to Eight Months

"I found this span of time a wonderful experience. My daughter continually surprised me with her growing abilities. I had not known that a child this young could be interested in a book. When my daughter received her first book from a friend, I was amazed to notice her interest in that book."

INTRODUCTION

Infants, on average, double their birth weight by the time they are five months old. They continue to gain body fat, which helps them to regulate their body temperature. This body fat also gives infants their "chubby" appearance.

Infants become more and more individualistic during the four- to eight-month period, and their permanent eye colour is established.

Many skills are gained during these four months, and differences in abilities and interests become more apparent as the infant grows and develops. These differences are evidenced by how soon they reach various milestones and how quickly they master various skills.

Infants' alert times are filled with activities that include manipulation, observation, and imitation of gestures and activities that they have observed. Increased control over hand and arm motions increases an infant's ability to deliberately act upon the environment by such actions as picking up small items and examining them.

Increased mobility, such as rolling and sitting, adds new perspectives to the infant's world. Infants develop a greater independence—they can grasp items placed near them and can roll over to reach an object. This increased motor ability, combined with better balance, provides infants with the opportunity to see their world from a new perspective. Until this point, the infant's view had been limited to what could be seen while lying on the back or tummy or while being carried. Now, a full visual range from a sitting position is possible.

Social interactions increase with the child's increased ability to initiate interactions and activities, communicate more effectively, and respond appropriately to a variety of stimuli within the social environment.

PHYSICAL DESCRIPTION

Infants continue to grow and develop at a steady pace during this period, with a continual increase in motor activity leading to increased body strength. The infants' physical appearance changes as teeth emerge and hair begins to grow and thicken.

TABLE 3.1	Physical Description—4 to 8 Months	
CHARACTERISTIC	**DESCRIPTION**	✳ **DEVELOPMENTAL ALERT**
Weight	Average gain: 2.2 kg per month	• No weight gain • Sudden changes in weight
Size	• Average gain: 1.3 cm per month • Average size: 69.8–73.7 cm	No continued change in size
Body proportions	• Head and chest circumferences are virtually equal • Head circumference continues to increase about 0.95 cm per month for 2 to 3 months; after the sixth or seventh month, head circumference continues to increase 0.47 cm per month • Legs start to lengthen but still have a bowed appearance	• Head circumference does not increase • Increase in head size indicates healthy brain development

TABLE 3.1 **Physical Description—4 to 8 Months** *(continued)*

CHARACTERISTIC	DESCRIPTION	✳ DEVELOPMENTAL ALERT
Respiration	25–30 breaths per minute; rate varies from individual to individual but is also dependent on activity	• Irregular breathing • Periods of not breathing at all
Teeth	• Cultural and individual variations (e.g., Black infant's first tooth at 4 months on average; Caucasian infant's first tooth at 6 months on average. Some children do not get first teeth until 1 year) • After the first tooth, a new tooth appears about every 2 months • During teething, gums appear swollen and sore, infant may be cranky, drool a lot, and continually bite, chew, or mouth objects	Tooth decay
Changes in reflexes	• Established reflex—blinking • Voluntary reflex—sucking • New reflex—parachute reflex: When infant is held face down and suddenly lowered, will immediately extend arms • Swallowing reflex has been refined—tongue is used to push food to the back of the throat	No change in reflex patterns

PHYSICAL DEVELOPMENT

As infants gain more control over their bodies, they begin to engage in more self-initiated activities. Alert times are filled with activities as infants manipulate toys and other objects.

TABLE 3.2 Gross Motor Development—4 to 8 Months

SKILL	DESCRIPTION	✳ DEVELOPMENTAL ALERT
Balance	• Sits without support • Reaches for items within range to retrieve them without falling • Balances in crawl position and rocks (Photo 3.1)	Frequently falls even when sitting with support
Sitting	By 6 months, sits without support—in high chair, on floor	Needs support to sit
Mobility	• Rolls in all directions • May roll to move toward a point of interest • May scoot backward by pushing with feet while on back	Minimal attempts to roll
Standing	• By 8 months, stands with support or holding onto furniture (Photo 3.2) • Bounces when held in standing position • 6–9 months: Pulls self up to standing position	Legs collapse when infant is pulled to a stand

Table 3.2 continues on next page

TABLE 3.2	Gross Motor Development—4 to 8 Months	
SKILL	**DESCRIPTION**	✳ **DEVELOPMENTAL ALERT**
Reaching	Reaches for objects or individuals, stretching out both arms simultaneously	Minimal reaching
Strength	Can lift head and look around when lying on back	Head not lifted

pincer grasp
the thumb and forefinger are used in opposition to pick up objects

palmar grasp
the hand and fingers move as one unit to pick up items

TABLE 3.3	Fine Motor Development—4 to 8 Months	
SKILL	**DESCRIPTION**	✳ **DEVELOPMENTAL ALERT**
Grasping	• Appearance of **pincer grasp**—using thumb and forefinger in opposition to pick up objects—develops at the end of this period (Photo 3.3) • Reflex grasp weakens, allowing infant to use some control in releasing object to transfer it from hand to hand • **Palmar grasp**—the hand and fingers move as one unit to pick up item; some refinement occurs toward end of period as pincer grasp evolves (Photo 3.4)	Reflex grasp does not weaken
Manipulation	• Explores cause and effect through shaking and banging objects • Bilateral holding—holding and exploring objects with both hands; holding two objects at the same time • Holds object in one hand and explores object with the other hand • Uses hands to alter the shape and size of an object (e.g., ripping or crushing paper) • Pulls off socks, hats • Undoes Velcro fasteners	Limited manipulation activities

PHOTO 3.1 The infant can balance and rock.

PHOTO 3.2 By eight months, the infant can stand with support.

PHOTO 3.3 The infant uses a pincer grasp to pick up objects.

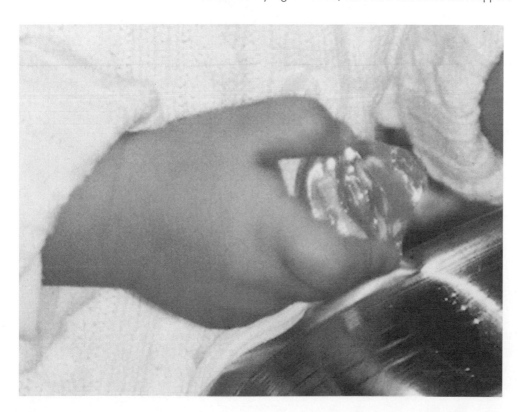

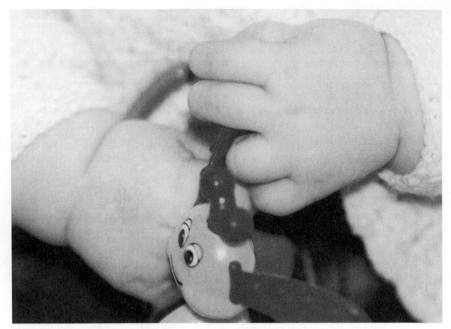

PHOTO 3.4 Hands and fingers are moved as one unit when the infant uses the palmar grasp.

SLEEP PATTERNS

Sleep patterns become more regular during this period, and infants usually sleep through the night for an average of 13 hours. Nap times are variable, but on average, most infants take a morning nap and an afternoon nap.

FIGURE 3.1 Brain Development: Reinforcement of Connections

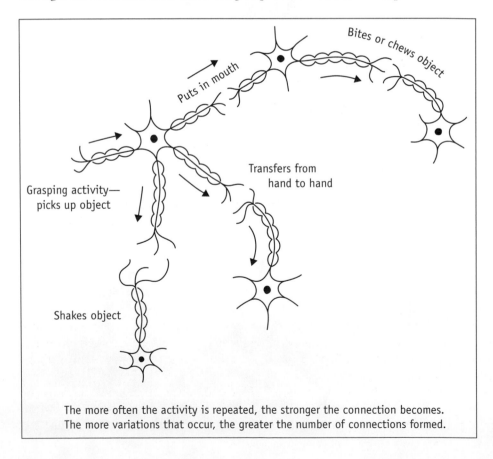

The more often the activity is repeated, the stronger the connection becomes. The more variations that occur, the greater the number of connections formed.

BRAIN DEVELOPMENT

The infant's brain continues to increase in size as myelination of the axons increases and additional connections are formed. Stimulation and a variety of learning experiences in all domains (physical, social, emotional, cognitive, and language) are critical to continue the process of creating and strengthening connections. For example, the more the infant manipulates, the more connections are formed and reinforced (see Figure 3.1).

SENSORY DEVELOPMENT

As infants' sensory skills increase during this period, they are more able to actively explore their world. Through sensory exploration, infants continually build on their knowledge.

TABLE 3.4 Sensory Development—4 to 8 Months		
SKILL	**DESCRIPTION**	✳ **DEVELOPMENTAL ALERT**
Visual	• Focuses on small objects • Long-distance focus sharpens • Eyes move in unison • Continued exploration using eye, hands, mouth • Depth perception—shows fear of falling from high places	• Does not focus on objects, irrespective of distances • Does not visually explore the environment
Hearing	• Can differentiate sounds (e.g., speech sounds from a knock on the door) • Increasingly good auditory discrimination • Prefers human voices, especially familiar ones—will stop activity, look at individual speaking, and react to what has been said	• Does not turn toward sounds • Does not react to sounds outside visual range
Touch	Skin, hands and fingers, and mouth sensitive to different tactile experiences (e.g., soft, hard, wet, smooth, bumpy)	No reaction to different tactile experiences
Taste	• May start solid foods • Individual food preferences develop • Food preferences, types of foods eaten are culturally determined.	
Smell	Increased response to pleasant or unpleasant odours demonstrated by facial expressions or body language	No reaction to different smells

EATING

Most infants start to eat solid food around six months. Feeding times begin to correspond with family eating times. Milk intake averages 177 to 237 ml per day, in three to four feedings. Infants begin to show interest in eating and start to demonstrate independence—turning away when hunger is satisfied or reaching for desired foods, for example. Infants' food preferences are usually related to their cultural backgrounds.

Care must be taken to present familiar foods and tastes to children at this age. Also, even at this young age, family members should interact positively with infants during mealtimes by labelling food experiences and modelling appropriate eating habits.

COGNITIVE DEVELOPMENT

As physical abilities develop, there is a resultant change in cognitive ability. As infants gain the ability to move, they also increase their ability to make choices, they become more independent, and they are increasingly able to understand the world around them.

object permanence
infant searches for an object that is out of sight or hidden and therefore gains an understanding that the object continues to exist even when not seen

trial-and-error learning
learning by trying different actions to get desired results

deferred imitation
spontaneously copying a behaviour or action seen previously

TABLE 3.5	Cognitive Development—4 to 8 Months	
SKILL	**DESCRIPTION**	**✳ DEVELOPMENTAL ALERT**
Emergence of object permanence	**Object permanence** develops in the following sequence: • Looks for objects that have been dropped • Searches for objects that are partially hidden	Does not look for objects
Preference	Actively chooses items of interest to play with if given choices (Photo 3.5)	Limited interest in play activities
Attention span	• Demonstrates boredom through body language (e.g., looking away, turning away, stopping the activity) • Demonstrates attraction to novel situations by looking at objects longer and/or manipulating objects	Limited attention span, irrespective of stimulation
Trial-and-error learning	Engages in **trial-and-error learning:** Tries different actions to get desired results (e.g., banging a lid on the floor, banging the lid on another object, or hitting the lid with another object)	Little evidence of approaching activities in different ways
Recognition of cause and effect	Demonstrates an understanding of cause-and-effect relationships through repetitive action, facial expressions, and vocalizations (e.g., while banging the lid on the floor, might squeal in delight and repeat the behaviour many times)	Little reaction to actions and results of actions
Imitation	• Observes an action (e.g., a caregiver clapping) and repeats the action • By end of this period, repeats at a later time an action observed previously (**deferred imitation**) (e.g., spontaneously waves goodbye when someone leaves)	Limited imitative behaviour
Memory	• Increasingly recognizes people, recurring events, and verbalizations, using body language, facial expressions, and vocalizations to indicate recognition • Recognizes common objects even when they are aligned differently (e.g., object is upside down or on its side)	Lack of demonstration of recognition

COMMUNICATION

Infants start to become more skilled communicators during this period, as they explore and produce different sound combinations. Their babbling sounds and body movements express feelings and intent and can usually be interpreted quite easily.

PHOTO 3.5 The infant actively chooses items of interest to play with if given choices.

TABLE 3.6	Communication—4 to 8 Months	
SKILL	**DESCRIPTION**	**✷ DEVELOPMENTAL ALERT**
Babbling	• Between 6 and 10 months, begins to string vowels and consonants together to produce sounds, such as "ba-ba-ba-ba" (this **babbling** includes the intonation and up-and-down patterns of adult speech) • Differences in speech patterns and sounds emerge	No babbling evident
Intentional communication	• Responds to own name and simple requests, such as "Wave bye-bye" • Imitates babbling strings, adult speech and intonation patterns, and nonspeech sounds, such as coughing or lip-smacking • Responds appropriately to variations in voice tone of others or to different auditory stimuli in the environment (e.g., laughing, crying, loud or angry voice, unknown or sudden loud noise) • Produces recognizable vocalizations to express feelings, such as anger, enjoyment, fear • Vocalizes during play activities	Limited communication

babbling
stringing vowels and consonants together in strings of sounds (e.g., "ba-ba-ba-ba")

TEMPERAMENT

Infants continue to use behaviour patterns established earlier but now have a wider range of ways to express themselves. How the infant feels and how the infant reacts to different situations are expressed through increased vocalization and a growing repertoire of facial expressions and body language. Consistent positive guidance will help the infant to begin to learn and use acceptable patterns of behaviour.

❋ DEVELOPMENTAL ALERTS
- Hard to comfort infant
- Many negative behaviours, such as angry crying or pushing individuals away continually

PERSONAL/SOCIAL DEVELOPMENT

In the four- to eight-month period, infants start to become increasingly more sociable individuals. Social skills are continually refined, added to, and practised. This growth in social skills is evident in infants' ability to:

- Observe other individuals and activities in their environment.
- Initiate contact through facial expressions, vocalization, and body movements.
- Express reactions to social situations through intonation patterns, body language, and facial expressions.
- Imitate appropriate social interactions (e.g., smiling, frowning, clapping, adult-like speech intonation patterns).
- Recognize strangers and react differently to a stranger than to a known person.
- Express displeasure at situations (e.g., when a favourite toy is taken away).
- Establish firm attachment patterns with primary caregivers.

❋ DEVELOPMENTAL ALERT
Lack of social interactions

EMOTIONAL DEVELOPMENT

The ability to express feelings provides greater opportunities to engage in social interactions. Infants are able to express their feelings through body language, facial expressions, and different types of vocalization. They also gradually learn to distinguish themselves as separate individuals. Increased skills are observed during this period in the following:

- Initiation of contact that has emotional overtones (e.g., initiating contact with a smile and accompanying happy babbling strings, or a sad face and tears).
- Ability to observe emotion in others (e.g., laughing in response to a happy face or sobering when the face appears to be angry) (see Photo 3.6).
- **Self-differentiation** (a process by which an individual gradually learns that he or she is a separate entity)—by six months, the infant self-differentiates but does not recognize the face in the mirror as belonging to himself or herself.
- Initiation of contact by body movements and verbalizations.

self-differentiation
process by which an individual gradually learns that he or she is a separate entity

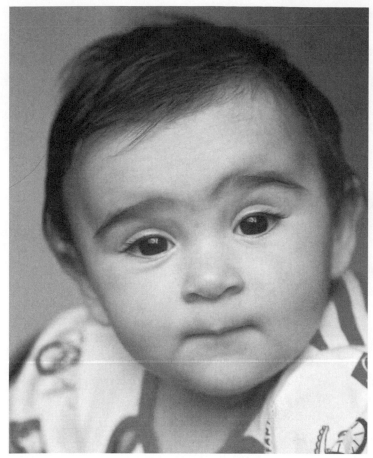

PHOTO 3.6 The infant looks sad observing the angry expression of another.

✳ DEVELOPMENTAL ALERTS
- Refusal to be cuddled or held
- Lack of initiation of interactions with others

PLAY

The development of play is cumulative. During this period, the infant uses skills previously gained and continues to expand these skills.

TABLE 3.7	**Play—4 to 8 Months**
TYPE OF PLAY	**DESCRIPTION**
Functional	Functional play—repeated play with toys to rattle, shake, or bang—practises existing or emergent skills
Solitary	Play involves increasing use of objects and toys
Sensory	• Objects and toys are manipulated, examined, put in mouth, and experimented with (banging or shaking) • Water activities—demonstrates enjoyment during bath by splashing and kicking, with appropriate vocalizations and facial expressions (Photo 3.7)

functional play
repeated activity to practise existing or emergent skills

Table 3.7 continues on next page

TABLE 3.7	Play—4 to 8 Months
TYPE OF PLAY	DESCRIPTION
Interactive	Rhythmic games with adults, such as being bounced, moving body parts in time to music, imitating adult behaviours, or initiating behaviour with an adult
Imitative	Increased repertoire of imitative actions and behaviours with use of materials

PHOTO 3.7 The infant demonstrates sensory enjoyment by splashing in the bath.

❋ **DEVELOPMENTAL ALERT**
Limited engagement in play activities

TOILETING

During the four- to eight-month period, the infant:

- Has an average of one bowel movement per day.
- Urinates more frequently, but female infants are drier for longer periods.

TOOLS FOR OBSERVING—FOUR TO EIGHT MONTHS

The following sample observation charts illustrate a simple way of recording the infant's various milestones, emotional development, and emerging and waning interests. Blank versions of these charts can be downloaded for your use from Nelson's Resource Centre for Early Childhood Education at www.ece.nelson.com.

SAMPLE 1
Developmental Milestones

A developmental milestone chart:
- Provides a record of development.
- Identifies developmental lags.
- Indicates the best experiences and/or materials for future development.
- Provides guidance for planning and implementing learning activities.

Developmental Milestones—4 to 8 Months

Name: Jennifer

SKILL	COMMENT	DATE
Gross Motor Skills		
Sitting	Placed into sitting position with pillow behind back	April 2
Rolling over	Rolled over from front to back	March 31
Crawling		
Standing with support		
Fine Motor Skills		
Palmar grasp	Picked up soft toys	March 23
Pincer grasp		
Manipulation skills	Transferred soft ball from hand to hand, looked at it, put edge of ball in mouth	April 2
Language Skills		
Cooing	Cooed all vowel sounds	March 22
Babbling	Used b, m, d in combination with vowel sound	March 30
Intentional communication	Babbled, stopped and waited for response, then babbled again	April 1
Social Skills		
Initiation of activities	Babbled sounds and waited for adult to imitate	April 1
Maintenance of activities		
Imitative behaviours	Then babbled back	April 1
	Waved goodbye	April 5
Cognitive Skills		
Object permanence		
Learning activities:		
Trial and error		
Cause and effect	Shook rattle/banged lids	April 4
Deferred imitation	Waved	April 5

SAMPLE 2
Emotional Development

It is important to identify the types of emotions expressed by infants in order to:
- Avoid behaviours that frighten infants.
- Build on positive experiences.
- Gain a better understanding of the child's emotional development.

Emotional Development—4 to 8 Months

Name: Yasmine

DATE	BEHAVIOUR	CIRCUMSTANCES
April 12	Yasmine started to cry as soon as she saw the frog move; when the frog stopped moving, she stopped crying.	New toy—green fuzzy frog dangling on a bungee cord from ceiling

Result of Observation

The frog was removed from the bungee cord and left on the floor within Yasmine's reach. She reached for it, grasped it, and put it in her mouth. Further observation might help to define just what frightened Yasmine in this situation.

SAMPLE 3
Interests

Identification of emerging and waning interests can help in planning new experiences and providing new materials for the infant.

Interests—4 to 8 Months

Name: James

DATE	INTEREST	CIRCUMSTANCES
April 1	Banged and shook things to make sounds— lids, block on floor, rattle	When several items were placed in front of him, he picked up items that would make sounds

FURTHER READING

Watson, L., Watson, M., Cam Wilson, L., & Crowther, I. (2000). *Infants and toddlers* (1st Cdn. ed.). Scarborough, ON: Nelson Thomson Learning.

Mansoor, J. (2005). *Infant stimuli*. Mississauga, ON: Infant Stimuli Canada Inc.

MINUTE EXPLORATION STAGE

Infants have gained more control over their actions. As a result, they become more attentive listeners and observers. They examine objects by exploring through looking, touching, listening, or moving objects repetitively in various ways.

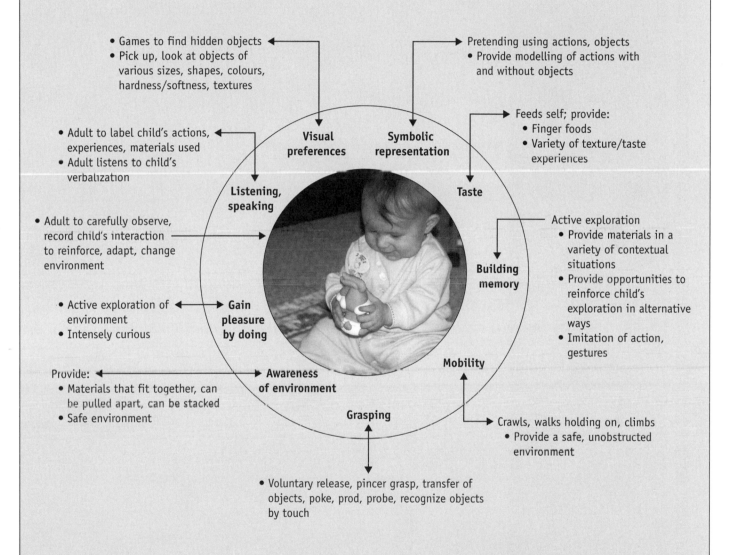

- Games to find hidden objects
- Pick up, look at objects of various sizes, shapes, colours, hardness/softness, textures

Pretending using actions, objects
- Provide modelling of actions with and without objects

- Adult to label child's actions, experiences, materials used
- Adult listens to child's verbalization

Feeds self; provide:
- Finger foods
- Variety of texture/taste experiences

Visual preferences

Symbolic representation

Listening, speaking

Taste

- Adult to carefully observe, record child's interaction to reinforce, adapt, change environment

Active exploration
- Provide materials in a variety of contextual situations
- Provide opportunities to reinforce child's exploration in alternative ways
- Imitation of action, gestures

Building memory

- Active exploration of environment
- Intensely curious

Gain pleasure by doing

Mobility

Provide:
- Materials that fit together, can be pulled apart, can be stacked
- Safe environment

Awareness of environment

Grasping

Crawls, walks holding on, climbs
- Provide a safe, unobstructed environment

- Voluntary release, pincer grasp, transfer of objects, poke, prod, probe, recognize objects by touch

CHAPTER 4

Eight to Twelve Months

Once an infant becomes mobile, the world becomes an exciting place. As infants actively explore their environment, they touch things, stop and sit to examine objects, put objects in their mouths, climb up and down stairs, walk while holding on to furniture (cruise), and seem to have endless energy.

INTRODUCTION

During this period, infants retain their chubby look. In fact, the amount of body fat peaks at about nine months. At 12 months, infants usually have tripled their body weight since birth. Boys tend to be slightly heavier and taller than girls. Muscular development also proceeds, with upper-body strength developing first. Infants become strong enough to pull themselves to a standing position. As they gain practice in using their lower body muscles, strength develops in their legs to prepare them for independent walking.

As their balancing ability and mobility increase, infants can explore the environment to a much greater degree. They can also now view the world from many different perspectives—from a sitting position, from a standing position, or from a caregiver's arms. Increased mobility also provides greater independence—infants are no longer totally reliant on adults to respond to every desire and can now get to desired objects or places by themselves.

At this stage, infants' abilities may vary greatly from one child to another. Some infants may already be walking by the time they are 12 months old, while others may still be crawling. Milestones are based on averages, and children's abilities may not follow these averages precisely. In fact, infants advanced in one skill, such as walking, may seemingly lag behind in another skill, such as talking, and be average in other abilities, such as manipulative skills.

Added dexterity of hand and fingers provides infants with a variety of additional options to manipulate objects in different ways, such as stacking items, pulling them apart, putting marks on paper, or banging objects together to create different sounds.

Social interactions increase as the interactions between caregivers and infants increase and are better understood by both. Infants are more able to communicate their desires effectively. Social skills are practised and expanded through many imitative activities.

Overall, infants become more independent at this stage in their development and are more interested what is going on around them. They also engage more in repetitive activities, which further expands their ability to control their actions and subsequently starts to build their awareness of their personal abilities.

PHYSICAL DESCRIPTION

Infants continue to gain steadily in size and weight. The upper body appears more developed, and the arms and hands appear larger in proportion to the rest of the body.

TABLE 4.1	Physical Description—8–12 Months	
CHARACTERISTIC	**DESCRIPTION**	✳ **DEVELOPMENTAL ALERT**
Weight	• Average at 9 months: 7–11 kg • Average at 1 year: 10.5 kg • Average gain: 0.5 kg per month	• No weight gain • Loss of weight
Size	• Average height at 9 months: 66–76 cm • Average height by 1 year: 70–80 cm • Average gain in height: 1.3 cm. per month	No height increase

TABLE 4.1   Physical Description—8–12 Months *(continued)*

CHARACTERISTIC	DESCRIPTION	✻ DEVELOPMENTAL ALERT
Body proportions	• Head and chest circumference remain similar • Anterior fontanel may close by 12 months, but average is 18 months • Arms and hands stronger and more developed than legs and feet • Legs still appear bowed	
Respiration	On average, 20–45 breaths per minute; rate varies among infants and is dependent on the degree of activity	
Teeth	On average, has four upper and lower incisors and two molars	

PHYSICAL DEVELOPMENT

Physical development progresses rapidly during these months. Infants become totally mobile and actively explore the environment using their increasing gross and fine motor skills. Items continue to be explored using all of the senses—manipulating things with their hands, fingers, and mouth; examining objects closely; experimenting with cause and effect (e.g., how to make sounds of varying types and intensities); and learning about different tastes and smells as a greater variety of foods is provided.

TABLE 4.2   Gross Motor Development—8–12 Months

CHARACTERISTIC	DESCRIPTION	✻ DEVELOPMENTAL ALERT
Balance	• While sitting, is able to grasp objects within range without falling over (Photo 4.1) • Pulls self up to stand and begins to stand with support (e.g., leaning on furniture) • On average, stands alone by 10–13 months	Poor balance while sitting
Mobility: Creeping, climbing, walking	• On average, creeps on hands and knees by 10 months; however, some infants do not creep before walking • On average, climbs stairs by 11 months • Walks while holding on to support provided by furniture or an adult (**cruising**) (Photo 4.2) • On average infants walk alone between 11 and 13½ months	No attempt to be mobile
Reaching	• Uses either hand to reach • Starts to point to objects at a distance	

cruising
walking while holding on to furniture for support

PHOTO 4.1 While sitting, the infant can grasp objects within range without falling over.

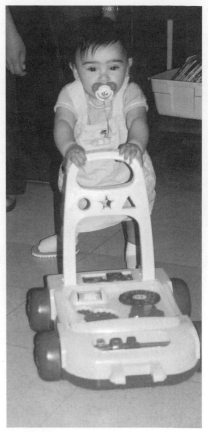

PHOTO 4.2 The infant walks while holding on to a support.

TABLE 4.3	Fine Motor Development—8–12 Months	
SKILL	**DESCRIPTION**	**❋ DEVELOPMENTAL ALERT**
Grasp	• Grasping reflex disappears at approximately 12 months • Voluntary release is developing—releases by throwing or dropping items • Pincer grasp fully developed	Grasping reflex still present
Manipulation	• By 9 months can perform two different actions with hands (e.g., using one hand to hold one popping bead while using the other hand to pull another bead off) • Stacks objects • Places objects inside each other • Transfers objects from hand to hand • Actively explores objects by poking and prodding	Limited manipulative activities

SLEEP PATTERNS

Regular sleep patterns have become established. Naps may decrease to one a day, usually in the afternoon. The infant may play quietly before falling asleep and more actively after waking up. A reassuring note for caregivers is that, after 12 months, sudden infant death syndrome is unlikely.

✳ **DEVELOPMENTAL ALERTS**
- Irregular sleep patterns
- Unable to fall to sleep, resulting in less sleep

BRAIN DEVELOPMENT

Infant brain development proceeds in a continual cycle (Figure 4.1). As the infant is stimulated to engage in new activities, brain activity increases. New connections are formed, and old connections are reinforced and strengthened. From approximately 10 to 12 months, neural activity of the brain increases significantly. During this period, it is critical for infants to receive stimulation in order to encourage active exploration of the environment with the support of sensitive, nurturing caregivers.

Stimulating experiences include activities to strengthen the attachment patterns—consistency in interactions and loving, nurturing relationships, attentive to the needs of the child; opportunities to explore and experiment; and appropriate learning materials and experiences. These types of activities ensure maximum "wiring" of the brain to provide the necessary foundations for all future learning.

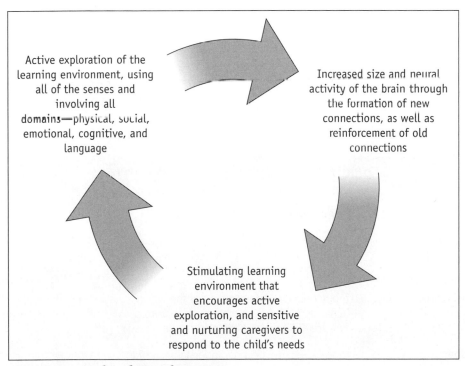

FIGURE 4.1 Cycle of Development

SENSORY DEVELOPMENT

Increased sensory abilities are evident in the infants' ability to identify and manipulate objects, actively explore their environment, make choices, and recognize familiar individuals in their lives.

TABLE 4.4	Sensory Development—8–12 Months	
SKILL	**DESCRIPTION**	**✳ DEVELOPMENTAL ALERT**
Visual	• Increased ability to identify objects at a distance; will point toward objects • Recognition of individuals from a distance demonstrated by body language, facial expressions, and vocalizations • Increased awareness of things and people when outside; will turn and stare	Lack of reaction to stimuli that are at a distance
Touch	• Hands and fingers used more to explore objects • Decreased mouthing of objects, but still common	
Taste and smell	Continuing increased awareness of different smells and tastes (e.g., sweet, bitter, salty, sour) as infant starts to taste more types of foods	

EATING

During the 8- to 12-month period:

- A daily routine of three meals per day starts to become established.
- On average, an infant requires snacks twice a day, once in the morning and once in the afternoon.
- The infant develops food preferences.

COGNITIVE DEVELOPMENT

Increased sensory abilities are evident in the infants' ability to identify and manipulate objects, actively explore their environment, make choices, and recognize familiar people in their lives.

TABLE 4.5	Cognitive Development—8–12 Months	
SKILL	**DESCRIPTION**	**✳ DEVELOPMENTAL ALERT**
Object permanence	Looks for and finds hidden objects (Photo 4.3.)	Does not look for objects if they are out of sight
Imitation	Demonstrates an understanding of the use of everyday items (e.g., pretends to drink from a cup or pretends to stir using a spoon and bowl)	Limited amount of imitative behaviour
Spatial relationships	Demonstrates an emerging understanding of in and out (e.g., puts an item into a container or removes it on request)	Does not react to request to put an item into a container

TABLE 4.5   Cognitive Development—8–12 Months *(continued)*

SKILL	DESCRIPTION	✳ DEVELOPMENTAL ALERT
Cause-and-effect relationships	Demonstrates a growing understanding of some cause-and-effect relationships (e.g., undressing a doll and giving it back to the caregiver to redress, or banging an object in different ways to increase or decrease the volume of the sound)	No evidence of an understanding of cause-and-effect relationships
Egocentric behaviour	Starts to demonstrate **egocentric** behaviour: • When something is wanted, it is wanted immediately • May pull someone's hair, not realizing that it hurts the other person	
Symbolic thought	Evidence of **symbolic thought**: • Holds up arms to indicate desire to be picked up • Crawls to the fridge and points at it to indicate a need for food	No evidence of symbolic actions
Sorting	At about 9 months, begins to sort into groups objects that have the same characteristics (e.g., toy cars into one group and toy people into another) (Photo 4.4)	No evidence of sorting ability

egocentric
sees the world only from own perspective, unable to understand another's

symbolic thought
using an action to represent a thought or idea

PHOTO 4.3 The infant can look for and find hidden objects.

PHOTO 4.4 The infant can sort objects with obvious characteristics, such as toy people and balls.

COMMUNICATION

Communication is a process that involves **receptive language, expressive language,** and **turn-taking** (see Figure 4.2)—listening, processing the information, and responding to the intent of the communication. During this process, there is natural turn-taking—listening, pausing to wait for a response, and responding.

receptive language
enables listener to understand what has been said

expressive language
verbal interaction or body language or gestures to initiate or respond to communication

turn-taking
listen to communication and respond appropriately, or initiate communication, listen, and respond appropriately

TABLE 4.6	Receptive Language—8–12 Months	
SKILL	**DESCRIPTION**	✳ **DEVELOPMENTAL ALERT**
Preference	• Interested in human voices, will stop and stare at the speaker • Listens intently to simple rhymes and songs, and moves to the music • By 9 months, infants usually prefer natural language that uses normal phrasing, with pauses between the thoughts • Prefers to hear native language used	Uninterested in human voices
Understanding	• Responds to some familiar words (e.g., "milk" or the name of a favourite toy or food) • Follows simple directions appropriately, such as "Give me one, please" (Photo 4.5) • Indicates "yes" or "no" by shaking head (not always consistent) • Looks toward source of voice when own name is called • Understands about 36 words at 8 months	Does not respond to familiar words, simple directions, use of own name
Native language effects	• Starts to use sound structures common in the language used by people in the environment • Gradual loss of ability to detect speech sound differences from non-native language; ability gone by beginning of this period	

FIGURE 4.2 Communication Process for Infants

1. Responding to a Stimulus

Receptive ————→ **Process Information** ————→ **Expressive**

Listens to stimulus: "Do you want some milk, Jamie?" → Jamie understands that he is being asked if he wants some milk. → Jamie responds by nodding his head and holding up his hand.

2. Initiating Conversation

Expressive ————→ **Response by Caregiver** ————→ **Response**

Jamie holds up his toy bear and says, "Ma–ma–ma?" → "Do you want me to hold your bear?" → Jamie smiles and holds up his bear.

Receptive
Caregiver listens to Jamie.

Receptive
Jamie listens to response.

Receptive
Caregiver takes the bear.

PHOTO 4.5 The infant follows directions to give something.

TABLE 4.7	Expressive Language—8–12 Months	
SKILL	**DESCRIPTION**	✳ **DEVELOPMENTAL ALERT**
Imitation and turn-taking	• Increasing ability to imitate sounds—mechanical sounds, babbling, cooing, tongue clicks, coughs, lip-smacking • Babbling takes on the intonation patterns of questions or statements • Uses babbling as well as more adult-like intonation patterns to express requests, along with physical actions (e.g., Christopher looks at his toy bear on the shelf, extends his arms toward the bear, and opens and closes his fingers as he says, "Ba-ba-ba" with an upward intonation. The caregiver retrieves the bear and asks, "Do you want the bear?" Christopher reaches out his hands toward the bear) • May listen to a song and then sing along, using a string of babbling sounds	• Limited imitation of sounds • Lack of turn-taking
Intentional communication	• Uses **proto-words** (e.g., "Da-da-da" or "Ma-ma-ma" are interpreted by the adult as "Daddy" and "Mama"); reinforcement of this interpretation encourages the child to use these proto-words in the accepted sense • Uses babbling and intonation patterns to get attention • Increases volume of vocalization, listens, and may increase volume again until a response is received	Lack of evidence of intentional communication
Gestures and body language	Increased use of gestures and body language to communicate; gestures and body language are individualistic and may need to be interpreted differently for each infant	Few recognizable gestures or body language used
"Real" words	By 12 months, an infant may have a repertoire of 2 to 6 "real" words	

proto-words
word-like sounds accepted as real words

TEMPERAMENT

The infant's temperament becomes much easier to identify as skills are developed that can be used to demonstrate that temperament. It is important to note that some indicators (such as a refusal to comply with certain requests or avoidance of interaction with strangers) are part of an infant's normal developmental growth. They are expressions of the infant's growing independence and awareness of the world. Normal developmental behaviours should not be confused with temperament.

✳ **DEVELOPMENTAL ALERT**
Major changes in temperament

PERSONAL/SOCIAL DEVELOPMENT

During this period, infants continually become more sociable beings, especially with caregivers, family members, and other familiar people. They are usually outgoing, enjoying social interaction and using communication patterns that are more easily understood.

stranger anxiety
infant clings to or hides behind caregiver or starts to cry when a stranger appears

separation anxiety
infant resists being separated from caregiver (cries, clings, refuses to let caregiver out of sight)

assertion of autonomy
infant begins to insist on independent action

social referencing
infant looks to adult for approval of an activity or behaviour

TABLE 4.8 Personal/Social Development—8–12 Months

DEVELOPMENTAL MILESTONE	DESCRIPTION	✳ DEVELOPMENTAL ALERT
Stranger anxiety	Demonstrates anxiety around strangers by clinging to or hiding behind caregiver, or by starting to cry (**stranger anxiety**)	No differences in behaviour toward strangers and caregivers
Separation anxiety	Resists being separated from caregiver—cries, clings, refuses to let caregiver out of sight (**separation anxiety**)	
Assertion of autonomy	Begins to insist on independence by refusing requests by crying or stiffening body (**assertion of autonomy**)	No assertion of independence
Reciprocation of affection	Identifies need for affection through body language (e.g., raising arms or crawling to adult and holding onto leg)	No initiation of affection
Social referencing	When engaged in an activity, looks back at the caregiver to seek approval (**social referencing**)	Little evidence of approval-seeking behaviour
Interaction with peers	By 10 months, starts to watch other infants; may initiate contact by vocalizing, smiling, crying, fussing	

EMOTIONAL DEVELOPMENT

Infants who have gained a sense of trust in the safety of their environment and the appropriate responsiveness of their caregivers begin to demonstrate control of their own behaviours and emotions. Infants may:

- Soothe themselves before to going to sleep by playing with their crib toys or babbling to themselves.
- Soothe themselves with a toy or activity after being upset.

- Stop taking part in activities that are no longer attractive or interesting by crawling away.
- Find new stimulation by exploring their environment.
- Engage in an activity for a longer period of time without adult interaction.

PLAY

Play activities become more social and more imitative during the 8- to 12-month period. Infants can make active choices and are motivated to try new activities or explore new materials and toys in their environment. Play is also repetitive, as the infant continues to practise emerging skills.

TABLE 4.9 Play—8–12 Months		
TYPE OF PLAY	**DESCRIPTION**	**✳ DEVELOPMENTAL ALERT**
Functional	• Puts objects into containers and takes them out • Takes things apart (e.g., strings of popping beads) • Pushes or pokes buttons to cause a reaction, such as causing a door to open	Limited play activities
Solitary	• Opens and closes things; explores cause-and-effect relationships • Plays alone before sleep or nap time	Infant needs adult stimulation to engage in play
Sensory	• Closely examines objects (minute examination) (Photo 4.6)—turns object over to look at all sides, feels object with fingers, pokes and prods to see what will happen • Demonstrates enjoyment of water activities (e.g., splashing, dribbling water, playing with water toys, soap, washcloth, nail brush) • Engages in repetitive gross motor activities (e.g., picks up a rattle and shakes it repeatedly; may stop and start this activity several times)	Limited sensory play activity
Interactive	• Plays games with adults (e.g., hiding and finding hidden objects, peek-a-boo) • Entertains adults by putting things on her or his head and laughing when the item falls off • Repeatedly throws things on the floor to have adult return them	

TOILETING

During this period, the infant:
- Has an average of one bowel movement per day.
- May be dry for longer periods of time or after a nap.

SELF-HELP SKILLS

Infants increasingly become more independent during this period, although their abilities vary greatly in this regard. In some cultures, infants are still carried by family members as the family members engage in work-related tasks, such as farming. In these cases, children are obviously less independent.

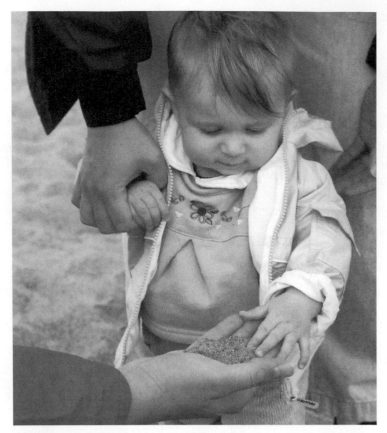

PHOTO 4.6 The infant closely examines objects (minute examination).

In Western cultures, infants are actively encouraged to explore and therefore tend to gain greater independence earlier. They are often more adept at feeding themselves and starting to initiate their own learning activities. Infants without those opportunities may be more placid and less inclined to explore.

TABLE 4.10	Self-Help Skills—8–12 Months	
SKILL	**DESCRIPTION**	✳ **DEVELOPMENTAL ALERT**
Eating	• Holds own cup to drink • Feeds self when eating finger foods • May try to use a spoon	No attempt to feed self
Dressing	• Pulls off clothes such as socks, hats • May pull down zipper • May pull off diaper • Starts to help in dressing process (e.g., puts arms into armholes)	

TOOLS FOR OBSERVING—EIGHT TO TWELVE MONTHS

Continue to use the following observation charts provided for Chapter 3:

- Developmental milestone chart (page 53)
- Emotional development chart (page 53)
- Interests chart (page 54)

Blank versions of these charts can be downloaded for your use from Nelson's Resource Centre for Early Childhood Education at www.ece.nelson.com.

SAMPLE 1
Behaviour

Completion of the behaviour observation chart can provide important indicators of:
- Types of behaviours you can expect from the infant in various circumstances.
- Successful strategies to use to soothe the infant.

This chart is useful for recording specific behaviours, such as separation anxiety or developing independence behaviour. Anecdotal comments (short, concise comments about a behaviour) may be added to document behaviours that do not occur regularly.

Behaviour—8–12 Months

Name: Kayla

DESCRIPTION OF BEHAVIOUR	CIRCUMSTANCES
• At 12 months, clung to her mother and cried when mother said she was leaving • Screamed when caregiver (Nellie) took her from mother • Nellie and Kayla went to window to wave goodbye • Kayla refused to be soothed for 15 minutes after mother left • Nellie took Kayla to book area; Kayla squirmed out of Nellie's arms, picked up a toy bear and a book, looked at the book, and stopped crying	Morning arrival at caregiver's; Kayla's outdoor clothes were removed by her mother, who filled in charts and then picked up Kayla to kiss her goodbye

SAMPLE 2
Identifying the Interests of a Group of Infants

The purpose of a group interest chart is to:
- Identify the success of the materials and equipment provided for the infants' use.
- Track the infants' use of available materials and equipment to adjust, expand, or adapt these as necessary for the infants' continued development.
- Use as an overall rating of the success of the organization of the infants' environment.

List the interest areas in your setting from which infants can choose. Record the number of times that you see an infant choosing one.

Group Interests—8–12 Months

Dates: Oct. 1, 2, 3

INTEREST AREAS	NUMBER OF TIMES CHOICE OBSERVED
Putting items in and taking them out of containers	|||||	
Looking at books	|||||

FURTHER READING

Watson, L., Watson, M., Cam Wilson, L., & Crowther, I. (2000). *Infants and toddlers* (1st Cdn. ed.). Scarborough, ON: Nelson Thomson Learning.

Mansoor, J. (2005). *Infant stimuli*. Mississauga, ON: Infant Stimuli Canada Inc.

REPETITIVE ACTION STAGE

Increased abilities lead to practice of existing skills and emergent skills through repetitive action in order to refine skills and abilities.

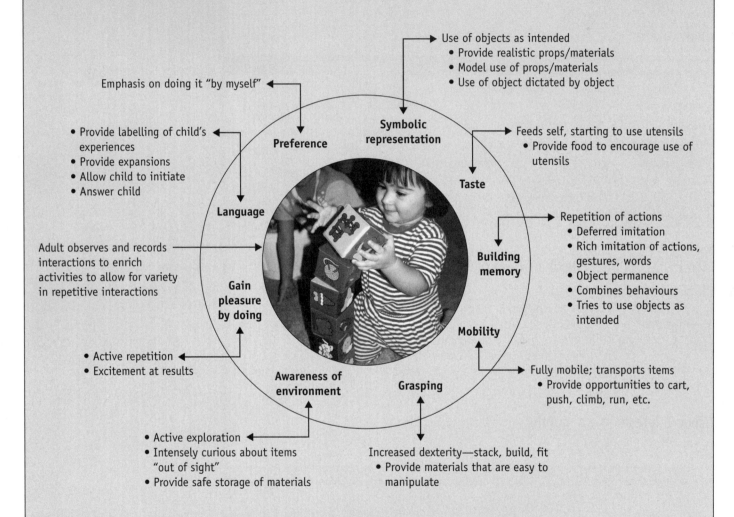

Emphasis on doing it "by myself"

Use of objects as intended
• Provide realistic props/materials
• Model use of props/materials
• Use of object dictated by object

Symbolic representation

Preference

• Provide labelling of child's experiences
• Provide expansions
• Allow child to initiate
• Answer child

Language

Feeds self, starting to use utensils
• Provide food to encourage use of utensils

Taste

Adult observes and records interactions to enrich activities to allow for variety in repetitive interactions

Gain pleasure by doing

Building memory

Repetition of actions
• Deferred imitation
• Rich imitation of actions, gestures, words
• Object permanence
• Combines behaviours
• Tries to use objects as intended

Mobility

• Active repetition
• Excitement at results

Awareness of environment

Grasping

Fully mobile; transports items
• Provide opportunities to cart, push, climb, run, etc.

• Active exploration
• Intensely curious about items "out of sight"
• Provide safe storage of materials

Increased dexterity—stack, build, fit
• Provide materials that are easy to manipulate

CHAPTER 5

Twelve to Eighteen Months

Infants in this age range exhibit a variety of behaviours that demonstrate their understanding of the world around them. They explore their environment to discover how things work, engage in trial-and-error learning (learning by trying a variety of methods to achieve a desired outcome) to solve sensorimotor problems, remember behaviours previously seen and imitate them at later times, and search for objects that are hidden.

INTRODUCTION

As infants grow and develop, individual variations in abilities start to become more obvious. At the beginning of the 12- to 18-month period, some infants—but not all—are walking, actively choosing their learning activities, using real words to communicate with others, and becoming quite independent.

Some variation in the development of these abilities is perfectly normal and should cause no concern—some infants just take longer than others to reach certain milestones. For example, Justin started to walk at eight months (he never crawled), while Christopher did not walk until he was 13 months old. Developmental growth variations may also be the result of differences in the following:

- Cultural influences: Infants growing up in Jamaica may receive specific physical exercises that are developed according to specific routines. These infants usually show enhanced motor skills development. In contrast, some infants raised in a rain forest in Paraguay are carried everywhere and have few opportunities to actively explore their environments. These infants usually are delayed in the development of many motor skills and may not walk until a full year later than infants given the opportunity to be more mobile (Schickedanz, Schickedanz, Forsyth, & Forsyth, 2001).

- Increased stimulation: Infants who receive appropriate care and learning stimulation usually show normal growth and development patterns. Increasing the learning stimulation, based on the infant's demonstrated abilities, can sometimes advance this process. In contrast, infants who are deprived of appropriate care and learning stimulation or are in abusive situations will show developmental lags in all areas, some of which may cause long-lasting difficulties (McCain & Mustard, 1999).

Developmental growth rate differences may also be a result of a special need. In these situations, special attention and expert help are usually required. In many cases, these are long-term conditions. Some examples are:

- Chronic illness and hospitalization: Development may be delayed because the infants spend a lot of time in institutional care where the appropriate stimuli cannot be provided; once released, these infants can catch up fairly quickly if the proper steps are taken to provide the needed stimuli.

- Conditions that affect normal development, such as cerebral palsy.

- Neglect and/or abuse: Infants who are continually neglected or abused may never catch up to their normally developing peers. (McCain & Mustard, 1999; Nash, 1997)

- Genetic abnormalities, such as muscular dystrophy (a disease typified by gradual weakening of the muscles, leading to loss of motor capabilities and eventual death) or Tay-Sachs disease (a disease that attacks the nervous system and may cause death by the age of four years).

- Accidents: Infants may have permanent brain damage due to falls or other accidents.

Infants in this age group usually develop at an amazing rate, mastering walking and communication skills, developing an increasing number of cognitive skills, becoming more independent, and demonstrating more awareness of others. Infants enthusiastically embrace learning, becoming active explorers in their environments and continually expanding their existing skills and developing new ones in all domains—physical, social, emotional, cognitive, and language.

PHYSICAL DESCRIPTION

From 12 to 18 months, the physical development of infants proceeds at a slower rate. The body shape starts to slowly change, becoming more adult-like in appearance but still top-heavy with a protruding stomach, responsible for the distinctive walk often referred to as the "toddler walk." In many cultures, the term "toddler" is used as soon as a child starts to walk, as opposed to most jurisdictions in Canada in which the age of a toddler is defined as being between 18 to 35 months.

TABLE 5.1	Physical Description—12–18 Months	
CHARACTERISTIC	**DESCRIPTION**	**☀ DEVELOPMENTAL ALERT**
Weight	• Average weight at 15 months: 9–13 kg • Increases 0.11–0.23 kg per month for the next few months	• Loss of weight • Overweight
Height	• Average height at 15 months: 73–83 cm • Average height at 18 months: 76–86 cm	No height gain
Body proportions	• Chest size becomes larger than head size • Head size increases an average of 1.3 cm every 6 months • By 18 months, anterior fontanel closes • Infant's bones harden to prepare for walking activities	Overweight
Respiration	22–30 breaths per minute; varies with activity level and emotional state	Erratic breathing
Teeth	By 18 months, on average, has a total of 12 teeth	Tooth decay

PHYSICAL DEVELOPMENT

The increased physical development at this age leads to greater ability to engage in a number of physical tasks. As infants gain more lower-body muscular strength, they are better able to balance themselves to sit, lean over, and grab a toy without falling and, eventually, to walk.

TABLE 5.2	Gross Motor Skills Development—12–18 Months	
SKILL	**DESCRIPTION**	**☀ DEVELOPMENTAL ALERT**
Balancing	• Initial attempts at walking are wobbly • Attempts to walk, pick up things while walking, or kick items may result in frequent falls (Photo 5.1)	No attempt to stand
Mobility	• May continue to crawl, pull self up to stand and cruise (walking while holding on to furniture), or walk (on average, walks by 15 months) • Climbs up and down stairs • Pushes or pulls toys while walking • By 18 months, usually can squat to pick up or play with toys (Photo 5.2) • Walk is flat-footed, with a wide, wobbly step	Limited mobility
Sitting	Sits on a child-sized chair	Lack of balance to sit on chair

PHOTO 5.1 The infant may fall frequently.

PHOTO 5.2 The infant usually can squat by 18 months.

eye–hand coordination
coordination of eye and hand movements to successfully pick up objects of varying sizes

TABLE 5.3	Fine Motor Skills Development—12–18 Months		
SKILL	**DESCRIPTION**	**✳ DEVELOPMENTAL ALERT**
Grasping	• Voluntary release established • Refinement of pincer grasp • Continued use of palmar grasp with some ability to use thumb in opposition to fingers	Voluntary release not established
Manipulation	• Coordinates eye and hand movements to successfully pick up objects of varying sizes (**eye–hand coordination**) • Passes an object from one hand to the other when offered a new object • Starts to put objects into a container and dump them out • Greater dexterity in using objects (e.g., crayons to make scribbles [Photo 5.3], a spoon to eat) • Drinks from a cup or glass • Uses finger to point to things, such as pictures in a book • Turns book pages • Throws objects in general direction of intent • Stacks items (Photo 5.4) • Picks up and carries items from location to location	• Little evidence of fine motor control • Inability to pick up and hold objects • Lack of interest in manipulation activities

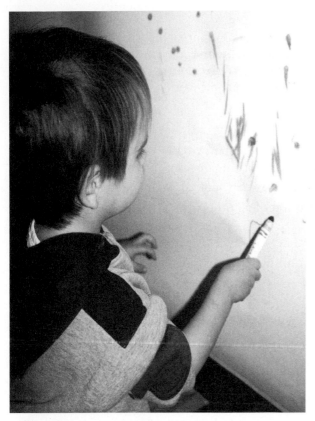

PHOTO 5.3 Improved dexterity allows the infant to scribble with crayons.

PHOTO 5.4 The infant can stack objects.

SLEEP PATTERNS

Between 12 and 18 months, the infant sleeps for 10 to 12 hours per night and usually naps once during the day. This age group is continually active and often finds it hard to wind down enough to sleep. Quiet, soothing activities, such as listening to a story or having a book read to them, may help infants to fall asleep.

❋ **DEVELOPMENTAL ALERTS**
- Irregular sleep patterns
- Long periods of cranky, hard-to-soothe behaviour

BRAIN DEVELOPMENT

There are two discernible periods of growth spurts in the brain. The first occurs around 12 months, coinciding with the time that infants usually start to walk and experience an increased capacity to make active choices. The second takes place between 18 and 24 months, during the time that the infant usually begins to use intelligible language. During these two phases of brain development, neural connections increase, leading to potential enhanced growth in all areas of development. This growth potential can be maximized by providing infants with opportunities to:

- Actively physically explore their environment.
- Actively use their senses to experiment with objects and materials.

Sensitive adults who provide a language-rich environment that encourages infants to communicate will make a major contribution to this growth.

SENSORY DEVELOPMENT

Infants' perceptual development in all areas is approaching that of adults during this period, and growth in all areas can be limited more by a lack of experience than by their sensory apparatus. During these six months, infants build the experiences that will help them to make sense of their world.

EATING

During the 12- to 18-month period, the infant's daily eating routine becomes firmly established and food preferences become obvious. The infant might:

- Be a "fussy" eater, disliking the texture, look, or smell of some foods.
- Prefer one food to the exclusion of all others.
- Demand to feed self.
- Have difficulty chewing some foods (e.g., meat, hard vegetables and fruits, which will need to be cut into small pieces) since not all teeth are present.
- Try to swallow foods whole (even smaller items, such as grapes, should be cut up to reduce the danger of choking).

COGNITIVE DEVELOPMENT

Infants continue to refine existing skills and to develop and strengthen new skills during this period. In all activities, infants demonstrate their growing understanding of their world.

TABLE 5.4	Cognitive Development—12–18 Months	
SKILL	**DESCRIPTION**	**✳ DEVELOPMENTAL ALERT**
Object permanence	• Becomes increasingly more adept in finding objects that have been hidden, looking for hidden objects in a variety of places • Demonstrates an increasing understanding of the continued existence of objects that are out of sight	Does not search for hidden objects
Imitation	• Imitation skills steadily increase • Uses objects for pretend activities (e.g., uses bowl and spoon to pretend to eat or cup to pretend to drink) • Imitates adult actions in play (Photo 5.5)	Limited imitative behaviour
Cause-and-effect relationships	• Shows increased understanding of cause-and-effect relationships (e.g., pulls a cord to cause wheels to spin or looks or moves toward the door when the doorbell rings) • Becomes more confident in ability to make things happen	Continues to use random manipulation
Egocentric behaviour	Continues to demonstrate egocentric behaviour (e.g., inability to share toys or materials with other children)	

	TABLE 5.4 Cognitive Development—12–18 Months *(continued)*	
SKILL	**DESCRIPTION**	**✳ DEVELOPMENTAL ALERT**
Symbolic thought and action	Increased use of gestures and materials to represent thoughts and ideas (e.g., placing hands at sides of the head to indicate sleepiness, pushing a block along the floor while making a truck-like sound (e.g., "Brmm-brmm-brmm")	Limited evidence of symbolic thought or action
Functional relationships	Demonstrates understanding of some functional relationships (e.g., socks go on feet, milk goes into a cup, a hat goes on one's head, a peg fits into a hole)	Little evidence of awareness of functionality
Sorting	By about 14 months, starts to group like objects together (e.g., all kitchen items or all bathroom items in one group)	Does not sort or group objects
Shape and spatial discrimination	Demonstrates awareness of shape by fitting certain shapes (shape discrimination) into holes in a shape sorter (spatial discrimination) (Photo 5.6) or placing single puzzle pieces into a puzzle form	No evidence of shape or spatial discrimination skills
Trial-and-error learning	When fitting a shape into a shape sorter or a puzzle piece into a puzzle form, twists and turns the item in each hole until it fits into one of them	Few attempts to manipulate items to find a fit

COMMUNICATION

A rapid increase in infants' ability to understand and express themselves takes place during this period, although their understanding of language is greater than their ability to express themselves verbally at this point.

The number of words understood in the 12- to 18-month age group varies from culture to culture. For example, Swedish infants are reported to understand fewer words than English-speaking infants at this age (de Boysson-Bardies, 1999). Even in English-speaking cultures, there are great variations, which might be due to:

- Physical maturation rate of infant.
- Health of infant.
- Caregiver/infant interactions.
- Language stimulation provided.
- Learning experiences provided.

PHOTO 5.5 The infant imitates adult actions.

PHOTO 5.6 The infant can fit shapes into a sorter, using the trial-and-error method.

TABLE 5.5	**Receptive Language—12–18 Months**	
SKILL	**DESCRIPTION**	✳ **DEVELOPMENTAL ALERT**
Understanding	• Identifies body parts by pointing to them • Points to familiar objects, people, toys, animals (Photo 5.7) • Responds appropriately to requests • Understands "no" • Responds appropriately to simple questions with "yes" or "no" and appropriate body language • Locates toys or familiar objects if asked to do so • Continues to listen to songs, rhymes, stories and might sing along • Understands familiar words that refer to routines, self-care, food, toys, objects around the house	Does not respond to simple requests or questions

TABLE 5.5 **Receptive Language—12–18 Months** *(continued)*

SKILL	DESCRIPTION	❋ DEVELOPMENTAL ALERT
Babbling	Babbling begins to sound like words—a combination of speech sounds and speech-like patterns	Limited vocalizations
Words	• Understands and responds appropriately to an increasing number of specific words for activities and objects • Understands about 126 words at 13 months and about 210 words at 16 months; this can vary greatly • Listens carefully while being read to and will point to pictures when asked or will spontaneously point to them	Does not understand many words

PHOTO 5.7 The infant can point to familiar objects.

TABLE 5.6 Expressive Language—12–18 Months

SKIP	DESCRIPTION	✳ DEVELOPMENTAL ALERT
Words	• Often uses animal sounds and sound effects, such as "yum-yum" along with actual words to describe games and routines, food and drink, people, body parts, animal names, clothing, household items, toys, vehicles, and prepositions (up, down) (Schickedanz et al., 2001, p. 207) • Easily confused by words that sound similar (e.g., dish and fish) until about 20 months	
Vocabulary size	By 12 months, average range of words: 0–52 By 16 months, average number of words: 40; average range: 0–347	
Gestures	From 1 year on, uses an increasing number of gestures in intentional communication, including: –**Deictic gestures**, used to communicate infant's intent (e.g., pointing at or reaching toward the desired object) –**Representational gestures**, which symbolize an object, a request, or a characteristic (e.g., a sniffing gesture could indicate a flower) (Schickedanz et al., 2001) –**Joint attention** process, in which the infant focuses an adult's attention on a desired object by pointing at it and then looking back at the adult to ensure that the adult is looking at the same object • By 16 months, pointing is accompanied by the joint attention process 65% of the time • By 16 months, is able to point at items at greater distances from self, irrespective of self's position in relation to the stimulus	• Few gestures used • Pointing not used
Language usage	• Uses **underextensions** (one word used for many meanings, such as "shoes" as a general term to mean all types of shoes) • Uses **overextensions** (use of one word to describe several different but somehow related items, such as use of the word "dog" to describe a cow because both animals have a tail and four legs). Both overextensions and underextensions disappear as children gain more vocabulary and learn the correct names of things • Uses **holophrastic** speech (one-word utterances that could be questions or statements, depending on the inflection used and accompanying gestures; for example, an infant could say "Milk" and mean either that he would like some milk or that his milk is all gone)	Small vocabulary combined with a lack of understanding of words

deictic gestures
gestures used to communicate the infant's intent

representational gestures
could symbolize an object, a request, or a characteristic

joint attention
process in which two individuals focus on the same point of interest

underextension
one word used for many meanings, such as "shoes" as a general term to mean all types of shoes

overextension
one word used to represent a broad category of items

holophrastic speech
one-word utterances that could be questions or statements, depending on the inflection used and accompanying gestures

TEMPERAMENT

An infant's temperament may be associated with how securely the infant is attached to the primary caregiver. Some of the results of studies of attachment behaviour patterns in infants aged 12 to 18 months appear in Table 5.7 (Schickedanz et al., 2001; Watson, Watson, Cam Wilson, & Crowther, 2000; Martin, 2003).

TABLE 5.7	Patterns of Attachment Behaviour—12–18 Months
TYPE OF ATTACHMENT	**TYPICAL BEHAVIOUR**
Secure Attachment • Separates easily from family members to explore toys • May cry when separating, but settles quickly • Prefers family members over strangers • Refers back to family member or primary caregiver to touch base	*Resistant Attachment* • Resists leaving family members to play or explore • Very distressed, cries, and is difficult to settle after caregiver leaves
Avoidant Attachment • Separates easily from family members to explore toys • No interaction with family members • No preference shown for family members over strangers	*Disoriented Attachment* • Inconsistent and contradictory behaviour patterns • Easily distracted • Erratic contact with adults • Lack of sustained activity or play

Healthy attachment patterns lead to healthy emotional development. Children who are securely attached tend to have a better self-concept and greater self-esteem, more readily initiate social activities with peers and adults, and find it easier to maintain relationships with peers and adults.

Self-regulation may be another factor related to temperament. When infants start to self-regulate their behaviour, they actively try to control both their emotional and physical responses to a stimulus. By the end of the first year, infants usually start to control their behaviour around strangers. By the time infants are about 18 months old, they have learned to take turns in play situations and social interactions.

PERSONAL/SOCIAL DEVELOPMENT

The increased motor ability and cognitive ability of infants of this age lead to a variety of emergent behaviours, such as empathy, interaction with peers, and assertion of autonomy.

TABLE 5.8	Personal/Social Development—12–18 Months	
SKILL	**DESCRIPTION**	**✳ DEVELOPMENTAL ALERT**
Empathetic behaviour	• By the end of the first year, starts to notice and respond to someone else's distress by crying, frowning, or looking questioningly at the primary caregiver • By 18 months, starts to do something about the distress—touching or patting the distressed individual	No empathetic behaviour observed

Table 5.8 continues on next page

TABLE 5.8 Personal/Social Development—12–18 Months

SKILL	DESCRIPTION	✷ DEVELOPMENTAL ALERT
Interaction with peers	• May start to play beside other infants if duplicate sets of toys are available • Develops strong sense of personal ownership—finds it difficult to share, may want to assume ownership of all toys	
Interaction with adults	Interacts with adults to show affection and get attention	
Assertion of autonomy	Increasingly wants to do things his or her own way and in own time; may refuse to cooperate in getting dressed or taking a bath	

EMOTIONAL DEVELOPMENT

Several milestones of emotional development take place between the ages of 12 and 18 months, including the following:

- *Reciprocal affection-showing:* Initiates and returns affection by, for example, kissing and hugging.
- *Empathetic response:* Implies an emergent understanding of others' feelings and recognition that others might need comforting.
- *Understanding of own emotions:* Begins to recognize own feelings of happiness and sadness.

PLAY

As infants gain greater ability to understand the world around them, their play behaviours also change. They start to experiment with toys and other items to make increasing sense of their environment.

TABLE 5.9 Play—12–18 Months

TYPE OF PLAY	DESCRIPTION	✷ DEVELOPMENTAL ALERT
Functional	• Repetitive play (provides skills practice) • Increased activity in putting items into a container and dumping them out	Limited functional play
Solitary	• Plays alone more often • Increased play with objects • Examines objects and toys to see how they function • Stacks items (e.g., blocks, two or three high) and knocks them down	Solitary play limited to playing with hands and feet; little evidence of play with objects
Sensory	• When filling and emptying containers with, for example, water or sand, runs the sand or water through fingers • Uses objects to make sounds—bangs, rattles, pounds, or shakes	Limited sensory play observed

TABLE 5.9   Play—12–18 Months (continued)

TYPE OF PLAY	DESCRIPTION	✳ DEVELOPMENTAL ALERT
Parallel	May start to play beside other infants using identical toys and in a similar type of play, but with no interaction (**parallel play**)	Not interested in other children
Interactive	• Continues to play games with adults (e.g., hiding and finding objects, imitating adults) • Points to pictures while adult reads a story • Tries to sing along when adult sings	• Limited interactive play • Play usually initiated by adult
Observer	• Watches adults doing things • Watches other children	
Role-playing	• Imitates adult actions (e.g., sweeping the floor, washing dishes) (Photo 5.8) • Likes to dress up (wear Daddy's hat or put on an apron to clean)	Few imitations noted
Creative	Starts to scribble, making intentional marks on the paper	No interest in scribbling activities
Gross motor	• Uses riding toys, pushes self along with feet • Increased repetitive motor activities (e.g., climbing, swinging, walking while carrying objects, chasing items such as balls, starting to run)	Lack of interest in gross motor activities

parallel play
play beside other infants using identical toys and in a similar type of play, but with no interaction

TOILETING

During the 12- to 18-month period, the infant:

- Has more control of bladder and bowel movements; regular bowel movements become established.
- Has longer periods of dryness.
- May let the caregiver know when diapers are soiled.

SELF-HELP SKILLS

At 18 months, infants move into the toddler stage, and toddlers often become very insistent on doing things by themselves. They want to:

- Dress and undress themselves, as they become increasingly adept at doing simple things, such as taking off their own shoes and socks and putting on a hat.
- Carry out self-care routines, such as face-washing with a facecloth or hair-brushing.
- Eat and drink by themselves.
- Help put away toys.
- Help with chores, such as helping to sweep the floor or to set the table.

PHOTO 5.8 The infant imitates adult routines.

TOOLS FOR OBSERVING—TWELVE TO EIGHTEEN MONTHS

Blank versions of the observation charts in this section can be downloaded for your use from Nelson's Resource Centre for Early Childhood Education at www.ece.nelson.com.

SAMPLE 1
Combination Tool

Figure 5.1 shows how an infant's play activities can be tracked during this period. This easy-to-use observation chart can be useful in identifying a child's interests, preferred type of play, and attention span, and can be used to record activities over several days.

Steps for Use
- Fill in approximate time line as bar graph.
- Add type of activity.
- Add type of play.
- Add comments as needed.
- Add "repetition of play" above same play.
- Draw line to indicate end of day.
- Continue next day.

FIGURE 5.1 **Play Observation— 12–18 Months**

Jamie

Oct. 21

Time

100
95
90
85
80
75
70
65
60
55
50
45
40
35
30
25
20
15
10
5
0

| | | P | |
| S | P | S | P |

Beads in and out of container

Listens to story three times

Crayons to scribble

Sand play—sand in and out of bucket

Activities

Comments:
Book read many times. "Baby faces"—pointed at pictures; identified sad, happy, angry.

Key:
S – Solitary play
P – Parallel play

SAMPLE 2
Type of Play

The purpose of this chart is to:
- Identify milestones reached—parallel play.
- Identify the need for identical materials for each child to avoid confrontations (e.g., blue buckets and red shovels for both children).
- Identify the infant's preferred activities and interests (e.g., sand play: filling and dumping) to facilitate the planning of future activities or expansion of existing ones.

Type of Play—12–18 Months

Name: Sarah   **Date:** Oct. 22

TYPE OF PLAY	DESCRIPTION OF ACTIVITY AND TYPE OF TOY USED
Parallel	• Beside Jamie in sand box
	• Both children filled blue buckets with red shovels, then dumped out sand
	• Repeated activity 5 times

SAMPLE 3
Collections

Collections of various items related to an infant's development can provide both emotional and practical benefits. Looking back later over an infant's early years can bring many happy memories, while tracking the infant's progress can help today by indicating areas where efforts can be made to enhance the infant's continuing development or where help is required. Collections can include:

- *Artwork:* Drawings done at different ages provide an opportunity to track an infant's development progress (e.g., see Figure 5.2, where the 16-month-old infant made a fairly simple scribble in one colour; in Figure 5.3, two months later, the infant made multiple scribbles in three colours).
- *Photographs:* Illustrate milestones an infant has reached.
- *Audiotapes:* Provide samples of changing communication patterns and documents development of language over time.

FIGURE 5.2 Christopher, 16 months: Red scribbles

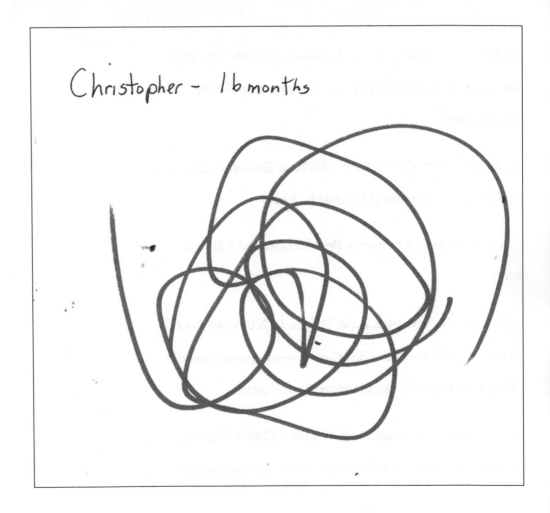

Christopher 18 months

FIGURE 5.3 **Christopher, 18 months: Blue, red, and green scribbles**

REFERENCES

de Boysson-Bardies, B. (1999). *How language comes to children*. Cambridge, UK: Cambridge University Press.

Martin, S. (2003). *See how they grow: Infants and toddlers*. Scarborough, ON: Thomson Nelson.

McCain, M., & Mustard, F. (1999). *Early years study: Final report*. Toronto, ON: Government of Ontario, Publications Ontario.

Nash, M. (1997, February 3). Fertile minds. *Time, 149*, 48–56.

Schickedanz, J., Schickedanz, D., Forsyth, P., & Forsyth, G. (2001). *Understanding children and adolescents* (4th ed.). Needham Heights, MA: Allyn & Bacon.

Watson, L., Watson, M., Cam Wilson, L., & Crowther, I. (2000). *Infants and toddlers* (1st Cdn. ed.). Scarborough, ON: Nelson Thomson Learning.

THE TODDLER YEARS

Eighteen Months to Three Years

INTRODUCTION

Toddlers are considered to be children aged 18 to 36 months in most jurisdictions in Canada. Toddlers are full of energy and bursting with curiosity, constantly on the move as they develop their autonomy and practise existing and emerging skills. Their continuous interest and enthusiasm about their environment leads them to:

- Stop and explore items of interests on walks.
- Empty cupboards to see what treasures they contain.
- Continually ask questions about things.
- Question the reasons for doing things.
- Take things apart and try to put them together again.
- Try to find out how things work.
- Engage in repetitive play activities.
- Engage in symbolic activities and play.
- Interact socially with peers.
- Be egocentric (seeing the world from a personal perspective—if the toy is in my hand, it is mine; if I see a toy I want, it also is mine).
- Become increasingly verbal and communicative.
- Demand to do more things for self.

Toddlers find it difficult to walk, climb, and run in a balanced, coordinated manner because their centre of gravity is above their navel. This makes toddlers top-heavy, and so it is harder for them to maintain their balance and move smoothly and efficiently.

Toddlers' activities are influenced by their background experiences and cultural expectations. For example, cultural backgrounds may vary in the degree of independence that is encouraged. Toddlers may, as a result, take pride in learning to do things for themselves or, conversely, may wait for adults to help them with tasks.

Toddlers actively explore their environment to repeatedly practise emergent skills to learn about their environment.

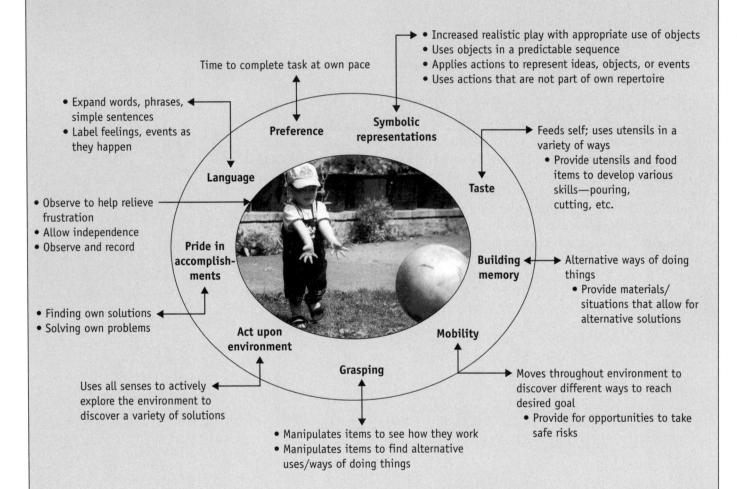

Time to complete task at own pace

- Increased realistic play with appropriate use of objects
- Uses objects in a predictable sequence
- Applies actions to represent ideas, objects, or events
- Uses actions that are not part of own repertoire

- Expand words, phrases, simple sentences
- Label feelings, events as they happen

Preference

Symbolic representations

Feeds self; uses utensils in a variety of ways
- Provide utensils and food items to develop various skills—pouring, cutting, etc.

Language

Taste

- Observe to help relieve frustration
- Allow independence
- Observe and record

Pride in accomplish-ments

Building memory

Alternative ways of doing things
- Provide materials/ situations that allow for alternative solutions

- Finding own solutions
- Solving own problems

Act upon environment

Mobility

Grasping

Moves throughout environment to discover different ways to reach desired goal
- Provide for opportunities to take safe risks

Uses all senses to actively explore the environment to discover a variety of solutions

- Manipulates items to see how they work
- Manipulates items to find alternative uses/ways of doing things

CHAPTER 6

Eighteen to Twenty-Four Months

"Christopher has such a vivid imagination. His play is full of imitation. A box will become a car, or a container a hat. His favourite toy is Cookie Monster. Cookie Monster travels everywhere with him. He tells all his secrets to him. Christopher is in perpetual motion. Everything fascinates him. I continually wonder at his energy and enthusiasm."

INTRODUCTION

By the end of the 18- to 24-month period, toddlers have, on average, quadrupled their body weight since birth. They have gained skill in communication and motor activities, are more independent, increasingly enjoy social interactions, and express their emotions more.

Toddlers engage in increased symbolized interactions and continual repetitive play, practising existing and emergent skills. Developmental milestone variations in these exist among toddlers in general and between the different skill levels of each toddler. For example, a toddler may be very proficient at symbolic play, have average ability in gross motor skills, and be advanced in his or her ability to communicate.

PHYSICAL DEVELOPMENT

The physical characteristics of toddlers have changed considerably by this point. Toddlers are starting to lose their baby fat and appear to be slimmer. Growth has slowed down considerably.

TABLE 6.1	Physical Development—18–24 Months	
CHARACTERISTIC	**DESCRIPTION**	**✳ DEVELOPMENTAL ALERT**
Weight	Average at 18 months: 9–13.5 kg Average at 24 months: 10–15 kg	• Significant weight loss or gain • No weight gain
Height	Average at 18 months: 76–86 cm Average at 24 months: 81–92 cm	No height gain
Body proportions	• Starts to slim down • Loses baby fat	

MOTOR DEVELOPMENT

Rapid growth in motor development occurs during this period, as toddlers start to refine and practise both gross motor and fine motor skills. Toddlers explore the environment actively through walking, running, climbing, and manipulation. Since toddlers do not have a concept of personal safety, they may engage in explorations that are potentially dangerous. For example, Darren, a 22-month-old toddler, wanted to reach something on the adult-height counter in the playroom. He climbed up onto the sliding rocking chair near the counter and then tried to climb onto the top of the back of the rocker. The chair started to move. Luckily, an alert caregiver was there to catch him as he fell.

TABLE 6.2	Gross Motor Development—18–24 Months	
SKILL	**DESCRIPTION**	**✳ DEVELOPMENTAL ALERT**
Balancing	• Squats to observe others or to pick up items • May try to stand on one foot for a short time • May try to stand or walk on tiptoes for a short time	Poor balance

TABLE 6.2 **Gross Motor Development—18–24 Months** *(continued)*

SKILL	DESCRIPTION	✳ DEVELOPMENTAL ALERT
Walking/running	• Uses wide-stance and heel-to-toe pattern; moves backward and sideways • Walking and running become more smooth and more refined • Increased ability to manoeuvre around obstacles (Photo 6.1) • By two years, is able to walk or run and come to a stop more quickly	No attempt to walk independently
Climbing	• Climbs actively without realization of potential dangers • Climbs everything, including chairs, furniture, climbing apparatus, boxes, large blocks • Climbs stairs one foot at a time	Limited interest in climbing
Riding toys	• Actively uses riding toys to push self along • Will use a tricycle, but will push it with feet rather than use pedals to propel it (Photo 6.2)	Not attempted
Jumping	• Jumps on the spot • May jump down from low objects (Photo 6.3)	No evidence of jumping

PHOTO 6.1 The toddler's ability to avoid or go around obstacles has improved.

PHOTO 6.2 The toddler pushes her tricycle with her feet rather than pedal it.

PHOTO 6.3 Toddlers may jump down from low objects.

TABLE 6.3	Fine Motor Development—18–24 Months	
SKILL	**DESCRIPTION**	**✳ DEVELOPMENTAL ALERT**
Ball skills	• Rolls balls and chases them, especially large balls • Catches large balls with two hands • Tries to kick balls	Does not attempt to play with balls
Manipulation	• Uses self-help skills (e.g., does up buttons, pulls up zippers) • Fills and dumps containers during sand and water activities; helps pour own milk or juice • Strings beads on pipe cleaner or plastic cord (Photo 6.4) • Stacks blocks • Turns pages	Limited manipulation of materials
Creative activities	• Uses both gross and fine motor skills to draw or paint • Draws using crayons or markers • Paints on paper or does finger-painting • Pastes paper, pictures, and other decorative materials on surfaces • Moulds dough	Limited creative activities observed; does not attempt any drawing or painting
Artwork (scribbling)	• Uses kinesthetic manipulation and expressive behaviours • Uses large arm movements and palmar grasp to create lines and circular shapes (Crowther, 2003; Schirrmacher, 2002) (Photo 6.5)	

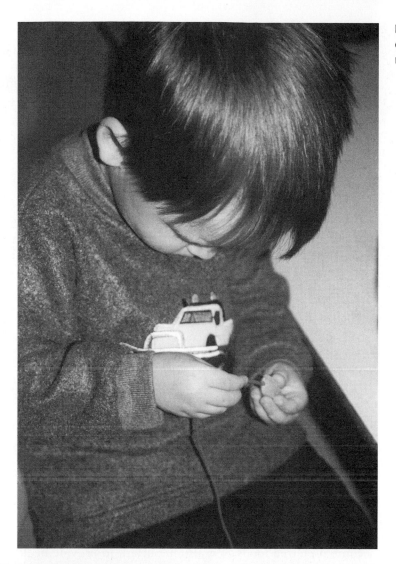

PHOTO 6.4 Stringing beads is an example of the toddler's increased manipulation ability.

PHOTO 6.5 The toddler's art shows her ability to use large arm movements and the palmar grasp.

SLEEP PATTERNS

By 18 months, the toddler sleeps an average of 13.5 hour per day, divided into about 11 hours per night and 2.5 hours during the day. By the time the toddler is two, the average sleeping time is 13 hours per day, divided into 11 hours of sleep at night and 2 hours of sleep during the day.

✳ **DEVELOPMENTAL ALERT**
Irregular sleep patterns

BRAIN DEVELOPMENT

A brain growth spurt occurs between 18 and 24 months. This coincides with the toddler's enormous language growth at this age and results in the "wiring" of the brain that ensures continued and vital language growth and efficiency.

EATING

By the time toddlers are two years, many food preferences have become established, and they have definite food likes and dislikes. Toddlers should not be forced to eat something they do not like. Dislikes may be associated with the following food characteristics:

- *Texture:* The toddler may not like the feeling of the food on the tongue (e.g., peanut butter because it is sticky).
- *Smell:* New foods with particularly strong smells, such as fish and cabbage, may be rejected by the toddler.
- *Appearance:* The toddler may not like a particular colour and therefore refuse to eat anything of that colour.
- *Arrangement:* Foods may need to be arranged on a plate in a certain way (e.g., different foods on a plate should not touch each other).

Junk foods should be avoided when possible because they can too easily become preferred foods. It is also important to provide healthy snacks.

Toddlers are very active and need to drink plenty of fluids to replenish the water loss due to their high activity levels, especially when outside.

COGNITIVE DEVELOPMENT

Toddlers' cognitive development is evident in their ability to search for hidden objects, use objects symbolically, use language increasingly effectively, engage in pretend activities, and recognize similarities and differences.

TABLE 6.4	Cognitive Development—18–24 Months	
SKILL	**DESCRIPTION**	✳ **DEVELOPMENTAL ALERT**
Object permanence	Realizes that when an object is out of sight, it still exists; will look for an object that is hidden	Limited evidence of object permanence

TABLE 6.4　Cognitive Development—18–24 Months (continued)

SKILL	DESCRIPTION	❉ DEVELOPMENTAL ALERT
Representational thought	• Uses symbols to represent objects (e.g., pictures representing objects) • Starts to understand that a symbol is separate from the object (e.g., the picture only looks like the object), and the object can be matched to the picture	Symbols not used
Pretend play	• Uses imitation and deferred imitation to act out roles, situations (**pretend play**) • Demonstrates ability to look at things from different perspectives, leading to a decrease in egocentric thinking	Pretend play not evident
Integrated thought	Connects symbolic ideas acquired in one area to another area (e.g., matching a toy dog to a picture, then observing a picture of a dog in a book and matching the toy dog to that picture of a dog)	Inability to connect symbol to a real object
Memory	• Is able to recall past ideas, events (e.g., remembers how to make a toy spin) • Increasingly recognizes and uses some words • Remembers words and associates words with actions, places, people, or objects	Little evidence of recall and use of past experiences
Making associations	Links two things together in mind (e.g., understands that sand toys belong in the sand box and books belong on a shelf or that throwing balls should be done outside or in the gym, but not inside)	Does not make associations between things
Sorting	Increasingly able to identify things that belong together (e.g., items of clothing, or toys, such as blocks or crayons)	Limited sorting ability
Trial-and-error learning	Increasingly applies past general and trial-and-error learning to new situations (e.g., putting shapes into the correct slots of a familiar shape sorter but resorting to trial-and-error learning for a different shape sorter) (Photo 6.6)	Few attempts to try to solve challenges

pretend play
use of imitation and deferred imitation to act out roles or situations

COMMUNICATION

From 18 to 24 months, toddlers usually begin to use words in combinations. At the beginning of this period, utterances may consist of only two words to express meaning, but by the end of this period, many toddlers use multi-word utterances.

Examples of toddlers' two-word expressions at this stage are given below (adapted from Schickedanz, Schickedanz, Forsyth, & Forsyth, 2001, p. 213):

- *Identification of items:* "My dog," "Look, train!"
- *Identification of a specific location:* "Me here," "Bear, bed"
- *Nonexistence:* "No more," "All gone"
- *Negation:* "No sock," "No ball"
- *Ownership:* "My dog," "Mommy's cup"

PHOTO 6.6 The toddler uses trial and error to put shapes together.

- *Recurrence:* Requesting more or for something to happen again: "More milk," "Do again"
- *Simple sentences:* Agent, action, object: "Daddy eat," "Eat cookie"
- *Attribution:* Describing or assigning a characteristic to something: "Red ball," "Big car"
- *Question:* "Where go?" What that?"

TABLE 6.5	Language Development—18–24 Months	
SKILL	**DESCRIPTION**	**✳ DEVELOPMENTAL ALERT**
Receptive language	Continues to understand more than is expressed	Limited verbal understanding
Telegraphic speech	Uses speech that resembles sentences but uses only the essential 2–3 words (**telegraphic speech**): "Want more," "Go home?"	Slow verbal growth; few words used
Vocabulary size	At 20 months, average of 170 words with a range of 3–544 words	

telegraphic speech
speech that resembles sentences but uses only the essential 2–3 words

TEMPERAMENT

Some toddlers seem to experience a temperament change during the 18- to 24-month period. For example, a toddler who previously seemed to be very easy-going suddenly becomes quite temperamental. This could simply be the result of a growing desire for independence, which toddlers often express by:

- Refusing to do tasks, such as putting away their toys.
- Ignoring adult requests, such as continuing to play when asked to put away the toys.
- Responding with a resounding "NO!" when a request is made.
- Exhibiting temperamental outbursts, such as throwing temper tantrums when they do not want to do something.

These types of independence-assertion behaviours are a natural part of toddlers' development. They are learning to set boundaries on their behaviours based on the feedback they receive, and so it is important to interact positively and to reinforce positive behaviours. This is the way that toddlers learn to regulate their behaviour.

✳ DEVELOPMENTAL ALERTS
- Exhibits no behaviour changes in most situations
- Has erratic, unpredictable behaviour changes

PERSONAL/SOCIAL DEVELOPMENT

Toddlers are learning about their personal feelings during this period, and these feelings are often close to the surface. Their emotions may swing rapidly, as toddlers learn more about their world. At times, it might seem that toddlers in this age group are engaging in a power struggle as they try to exert their independence—ignoring adult requests, refusing to share, or adamantly demanding another child's toy. In most cases, however, they are simply expressing their desire for autonomy.

TABLE 6.6	Personal/Social Development—18–24 Months	
SKILL	**DESCRIPTION**	**✳ DEVELOPMENTAL ALERT**
Emotional control	• Increasingly displays feelings of sadness, happiness, fear, mistrust (e.g., of strangers, strange situations), or anger • May demonstrate negative feelings by crying, shouting, grabbing, or even hitting or biting, but does not understand what he or she is feeling or why he or she is feeling this way • Empathetic behaviour increases (e.g., stops play to stare at a crying child and offers the child a hug or a toy)	Hard to console or settle
Peer interactions	• Parallel play established (Photo 6.7) • Easily distracted by activities of peers and will run to become involved in the activity	Ignores other children

Table 6.6 continues on next page

TABLE 6.6	Personal/Social Development—18–24 Months	
SKILL	DESCRIPTION	✳ DEVELOPMENTAL ALERT
Self-concept	• Recognizes self in mirror or in a photograph • Refers to self by own name • Uses personal pronouns—"me," "I" • Points to own and to someone else's nose, indicating understanding of self as being different from someone else	Does not recognize self in mirror or refer to self
Autonomy	Increased ability to be independent: Helps to dress self, eats and drinks without assistance, carries out self-care routines (washing face and hands, brushing teeth), puts away toys	Limited independent activity

PLAY

Toddlers start to become more aware of other children around them. Their play increasingly becomes more symbolic and creative and involves pretending and exploration of objects. Cultural sensitivity may be observed in toddler play. For example, in Senegal, toddlers' roles are already defined as male or female, and play revolves around household chores for girls (e.g., pounding wheat) and hunting or vehicle-related activities for boys (Schickedanz et al., 2001).

PHOTO 6.7 The toddler's ability to parallel play is established.

TABLE 6.7 Play—18–24 Months

TYPE OF PLAY	DESCRIPTION	✳ DEVELOPMENTAL ALERT
Parallel	Parallel play established as regular part of toddler play	Only solitary play observed
Pretend	• Pretend play dictated by objects that are available (e.g., if a doll and toy bottle are on hand, will feed the doll) • Pretend play revolves around familiar experiences (e.g., walking a dog, feeding or bathing a baby, preparing a meal) (Photo 6.8)	Limited pretend play
Creative	• Begins to name items created with toys (e.g., buildings made with blocks) • Scribbles feature more varied forms (e.g., could include straight lines, curved lines, dots, circles) • Uses more colours • Draws and scribbles with intent; names what has been drawn • Accidental mixing of colours may lead to intentional mixing • Experiments with musical instruments to create various sounds, volumes, rhythms	Little evidence of creativity or individuality
Symbolic	• Increasingly uses one item as a subsitute for another (e.g., a block may become a car or a telephone) • May take shapes of objects into account during symbolic play (e.g., may use curved block to represent a telephone or a straight stick as a stirrer)	Limited symbolic play
Functional	• Tends to focus on activities that involve emptying, filling, taking apart, stacking, knocking down	Limited manipulation ability
Block	Carries and stacks blocks	No block play observed

TOILETING

Toddlers may show signs of readiness to be toilet trained around 24 months, but this could occur earlier or later. Toilet training should not be a forced activity and should be fun for the toddler. Some of the signs that a toddler is ready for toilet training are as follows:

- Shows an interest in toileting activities
- Understands what is happening
- Can control the muscles that regulate urination and bowel movement
- Talks about bowel and bladder movements ("I peed")
- Is frequently dry for two hours or more
- Indicates toilet need by stopping play and holding self or by telling someone
- Pulls up own pants
- Asks to be changed when wet or dirty

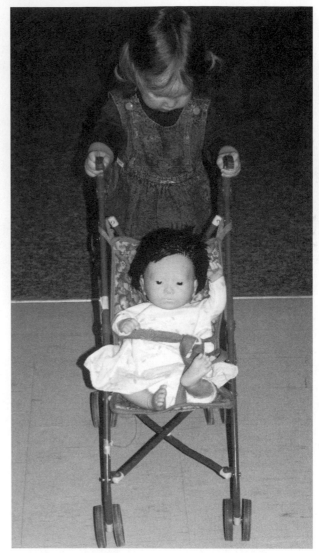

PHOTO 6.8 The toddler's pretend play mainly involves familiar experiences, such as walking a baby.

SELF-HELP SKILLS

Toddlers demand to do things by themselves. It is important to help them achieve more independence by adapting situations to make it easier for them to be self-reliant. For example, clothing that has snaps or shoes that have Velcro fasteners could be provided. Toddlers also love to help. Child-sized cleaning materials facilitate establishing routines, such as sweeping up spills or cleaning dirty tabletops.

Toddlers also refine their self-help skills during this period, such as hand and face washing. Supervision is required, as they are easily distracted by various aspects of an activity and may forget what was intended. For example, as toddlers wash their hands, they may become distracted by the sensory aspect of the water and forget to rinse the soap off their skin.

TABLE 6.8	Self-Help Skills—18–24 Months	
SKILL	**DESCRIPTION**	**✳ DEVELOPMENTAL ALERT**
Dressing	• Increased ability and desire to dress self (e.g., put on own shirt, sweater, or shoes) • Can do part of some routines without help (e.g., pulling up a zipper if it is started, putting on own shoes if shoes are held in place)	No attempt to dress self
Eating	• Feeds self using spoon; starts to use fork • Drinks without assistance but may still spill	Lack of interest in feeding self
Self-care	• Washes own face and hands but requires supervision • Brushes own teeth but requires reminders about what motion to use and where to brush • Combs hair while looking in mirror at self	Lack of interest in self-care
Clean-up	• Helps put away toys • Helps clean tabletops and floor but requires supervision	Limited interest in cleaning up

TOOLS FOR OBSERVING—18–24 MONTHS

Blank versions of the charts below can be downloaded for your use from Nelson's Resource Centre for Early Childhood Education at www.ece.nelson.com.

SAMPLE 1
Language Usage

The language usage observation chart below can be used to identify:
- Milestones reached.
- Development areas where skills need reinforcement or expansion.
- Materials to provide reinforcement and expansion of skills.

See pages **99–100** for examples of each language usage category listed in the chart.

Language Usage—18–24 Months

Name: Dates:

CATEGORY	DESCRIPTION
Identification of items	
Identification of specific location	
Nonexistence	
Negation	
Ownership	
Recurrence	
Simple sentences	
Attribution	
Question	

SAMPLE 2

Toilet Training Readiness Checklist—18–24 Months

Name: Dates:

READINESS SIGNS	FREQUENCY	COMMENTS
• Talks about toileting ("I peed," "Poop smells")		
• Dry for two hours or more		
• Demonstrates need		
• Pulls pants down and up		
• Asks to be changed when dirty or wet		

REFERENCES

Crowther, I. (2003). *Creating effective learning environments*. Scarborough, ON: Nelson Thomson Learning.

Schickedanz, J., Schickedanz, D., Forsyth, P., & Forsyth, G. (2001). *Understanding children and adolescents* (4th ed.). Needham Heights, MA: Allyn & Bacon.

Schirrmacher, R. (2002). *Art and creative development for young children*. Albany, NY: Delmar.

CHAPTER 7

Two to Three Years

During this two- to three-year period, children continue to expand on and refine the skills that they previously acquired and to develop new ones as they continue active exploration of their environment.

INTRODUCTION

The toddler's growth and changes in behaviour start to slow down in the third year as skills are consolidated and refined. Conflict is inevitable between adults and toddlers during this period, with the toddlers increasingly demanding autonomy. Although they often seem unwilling to do so, toddlers must learn to:

- Behave in an acceptable manner, balancing their need for independence with an appropriate level of compliance with adult requirements.
- Make appropriate choices (e.g., a spoon may be used to stir with, as a scoop, or to bang).
- Share ideas and materials.
- Solve problems (e.g., will try things to accomplish tasks without requiring help, such as dressing, pouring own drink, or finishing a simple puzzle).
- Practise emergent skills (repetitive play refines and reinforces emergent skills).

PHYSICAL DEVELOPMENT

The body proportions of toddlers in this age group are much more adult-like in appearance. However, their centre of balance is still lower than that of a pre-schooler, which gives toddlers a slightly unbalanced look as they walk and run—thus, the name "toddler."

TABLE 7.1	Physical Development—2–3 Years	
CHARACTERISTIC	**DESCRIPTION**	**❊ DEVELOPMENTAL ALERT**
Weight	Average weight at 24 months: 10–1.5 kg Average weight at 36 months: Four times the birth weight	Extreme weight loss or gain
Height	Average height: 86.3–96.5 cm	
Body proportions and posture	• Protruding stomach • Swayed back • More erect posture	Poor posture
Teeth	• Second molars develop • On average, has 20 teeth	Tooth decay or gum problems

MOTOR DEVELOPMENT

During this period, repetitive motor activities provide opportunities for the toddler to develop greater strength, endurance, balance, coordination, and flexibility, while refining previously acquired skills.

TABLE 7.2	Gross Motor Development—2–3 Years	
SKILL	**DESCRIPTION**	**❊ DEVELOPMENTAL ALERT**
Balancing	• Stands on one foot for a few moments before losing balance • Falls less frequently when walking and running • Squats with balance for long periods of time • Walks on balance beam for a few steps	Poor balance overall

TABLE 7.2 Gross Motor Development—2–3 Years (continued)

SKILL	DESCRIPTION	✳ DEVELOPMENTAL ALERT
Walking/running	• Has a more upright posture when walking and running • Walk is more refined—less of a wide stance, and increased heel-to-toe pattern • Navigates smoothly around obstacles	• Poor control when walking or running • Bumps into things often
Climbing	• Climbs onto chairs or platforms, then turns around to sit • Can coordinate simultaneous arm and leg movements toward end of period • By the end of this period, may alternate feet when climbing	Limited climbing activities
Jumping	• Jumps down from short heights (e.g., stairs or low platforms) • Achieves higher on-the-spot jumps	Limited jumping activities
Ball skills	• Throws ball underhand • Successfully catches ball with two hands more often (Photo 7.1) • Kicks ball while running and continues to chase and kick it	
Movement to music	• Rhythmically sways to music • Moves around to music, often following a steady beat	Moves erratically to music
Using riding toy pedals	May start to use riding toy pedals for propulsion by the end of the second year (**trundling**)	

PHOTO 7.1 Toddlers gain increased skill in catching a ball with both hands.

trundling
using alternate feet to propel a riding toy forward

TABLE 7.3 Fine Motor Development—2–3 Years

SKILL	DESCRIPTION	✳ DEVELOPMENTAL ALERT
Manipulation	• Has increased dexterity using either pincer or palmar grasp, holding things in one hand while using crayons or paintbrushes, and drinking from a cup • Readily fits items into proper slots (e.g., pegs into pegboard) • Takes objects apart and puts them together again correctly (e.g., Duplo blocks, nuts and bolts) • Can hit pegs on the head (e.g., with pounding benches) • Experiments with "safe" scissors (Photo 7.2)	• Inability to use one hand only • Limited manipulation of materials

Table 7.3 continues on next page

TABLE 7.3	Fine Motor Development—2–3 Years	
SKILL	**DESCRIPTION**	**❋ DEVELOPMENTAL ALERT**
Artwork	• Starts to cover a greater area of paper with scribbles and paintings • Experiments with paint, applying several layers • Creates drawings with scribbles of various sizes, colours, and shapes (Photo 7.3) *Disordered and random scribbling: 1½–2½ yrs.* • Uses large muscles and whole-arm movement • Uses whole-hand grip • Keeps wrist rigid • Uses minimal finger movement (Crowther, 2003, p. 199) • May use either hand to scribble • May not look at paper while scribbling • Creates haphazard lines • Makes a line with a single movement (Photo 7.4) • May scribble beyond confines of the paper *Controlled scribbling: 2–3 yrs.* • Makes smaller marks • Uses the same motion to scribble repeatedly • Starts to move wrist while scribbling • Watches intently while scribbling • Starts to use different types of lines going in various directions • Places lines deliberately in the middle, at the top • Produces wider variety of scribbles—more intricate lops and swirls • Uses more colours (Crowther, 2003, p. 200) • Stays within confines of the paper	Scribbling activities not observed

SLEEP PATTERNS

Toddlers sleep 11 hours per night, on average, with a two-hour nap time during the day. They usually play for longer periods before falling asleep and need a quiet time to wind down before sleeping.

❋ DEVELOPMENTAL ALERT
Irregular sleep patterns

BRAIN DEVELOPMENT

The brain grows to about 70 to 80 percent of an adult's brain size during this period, and the number of connections reaches adult levels.

EATING

During the two- to three-year period, the toddler:

- May have a fluctuating appetite; tends to eat a lot during growth spurts.
- Has definite likes and dislikes (e.g., dislikes mixtures of foods, likes familiar foods served in familiar ways).

PHOTO 7.2 Toddlers will experiment with scissors.

PHOTO 7.3 Toddlers begin to produce scribbles using different sizes and shapes of lines in a variety of colours.

PHOTO 7.4 Toddlers often produce a line with a single movement.

- Imitates table manners, which may be inappropriate or appropriate; good modelling of appropriate table manners should be provided.
- Has a high activity level and requires regular fluid intake and snacks.

COGNITIVE DEVELOPMENT

As toddlers explore the world around them, they gain increased knowledge of how things work. They start to label their actions and the things around them. Toddlers' play becomes rich in symbolic interactions as they learn to represent their actions, feelings, and materials through language and through representative actions and pretend play.

TABLE 7.4	Cognitive Development—2–3 Years	
SKILL	DESCRIPTION	✳ DEVELOPMENTAL ALERT
Symbolic function	• Pretend play is dominated by the type of objects provided (e.g., dishes lead to pretend eating, stuffed animals lead to animal role-playing) • Uses one object to represent another, dependent on the shape of the object (e.g., uses a seashell to represent a cup) (Photo 7.5)	Absence of pretend play with objects
Attention span	• Increased attention span for activities of interest • May return to an activity over several days	• Short attention span • Does not repeat activities
Cause and effect	Has greater understanding of cause and effect (e.g., knows that a toy must be wound up to operate or that squeezing a toy in a certain spot will make a noise) and uses this knowledge in play situations	Lack of understanding of cause and effect
Sorting	• Sorts like objects into categories (e.g., all cars in one group, all animals in another) • Starts to sort into more finite categories (e.g., all dogs in one group, all cows in another; all very large items in one group, all very small items in another) (Photo 7.6)	Limited sorting activities
Books	• Names pictures in books • Looks at books when alone • Asks to have book read out loud	Lack of interest in books
Concept development	• Develops simple concepts of time (e.g., before, after, bedtime) • Grasps simple spatial concepts (e.g., up, down, near, far) • Identifies quantities generally (e.g., lots, more) • Names, matches, and mixes colours	Limited evidence of concept development

TABLE 7.4	Cognitive Development—2–3 Years *(continued)*	
SKILL	**DESCRIPTION**	**✳ DEVELOPMENTAL ALERT**
Memory	• Remembers some words, people, events; demonstrated by rapid vocabulary growth, understanding of the use of language, recognition of adults, peers, and familiar objects by name • Repeats sequences of familiar routines (e.g., washing, dressing)	Difficulty remembering words, people, or events
Problem-solving	Solves simple problems (e.g., how to get down from a climber, how to find a toy that is out of sight)	No evidence of problem solving

PHOTO 7.5 Toddlers often use one object to represent another that is similar in shape.

PHOTO 7.6 Toddlers can sort objects into more finite categories (e.g., toy snakes in one group and dinosaurs in another).

COMMUNICATION

During this period, toddlers' increased ability to communicate leads to their participation in more complex social interactions. Their great curiosity about everything is demonstrated by active exploration of their environment and by continuous questions. Vocabulary acquisition accelerates with age, and toddlers learn at least one new word per day during this period. They continue to understand more than they are able to verbalize.

TABLE 7.5 Language Development—2–3 Years

SKILL	DESCRIPTION	✳ DEVELOPMENTAL ALERT
Language usage	• Expands two-word utterances to three or more words • Uses conventional word order in utterances (e.g., "Me go out") • Asks many questions (e.g., "Why?" and "What's that?") • Uses plurals (e.g., dolls, cats) but also generalizes grammatical rules to create words (e.g., mices, foots) • Starts to talk about events that have occurred in the past (e.g., tells daycare staff about what was eaten for breakfast at home) • May stammer • Uses language, not just noises, to get attention • Uses words to indicate when something hurts and to explain where the pain is	• Limited verbalizations • Does not cry as indicator of pain
Vocabulary size	• Average number of words at 2 years: 311 • Average number of words at 2½ years: 574; word range 208–675 words	

PERSONAL/SOCIAL DEVELOPMENT

Toddlers are becoming much more sociable at this age. They are aware of other children around them and they start to play near others, but still find it difficult to share materials or ideas. Toddlers are very curious; for example, when they become aware of activity somewhere else in the room, they often leave their own activity to see what is happening.

TABLE 7.6 Personal/Social Development—2–3 Years

SKILL	DESCRIPTION	✳ DEVELOPMENTAL ALERT
Emotional control	• Uses hugs and kisses to comfort others • Spontaneously initiates hugging and kissing activities with peers or adults • Grabbing, biting, hitting decrease as verbal competence increases • Finds it difficult to wait for something or to take turns (egocentric behaviour) • Negative behaviours, such as temper tantrums, peak during this year, then diminish with increased verbal competency	Lack of empathy toward others
Peer interaction	• Continues to be possessive of toys • Finds it hard to share • Observes other children play and may imitate that play • Continues to be easily distracted by other activities—rushes over to watch or demands to take part	Ignores peers

TABLE 7.6 Personal/Social Development—2–3 Years *(continued)*

SKILL	DESCRIPTION	✳ DEVELOPMENTAL ALERT
Ritualistic behaviour	Everything is done exactly by familiar routine (e.g., toys are always returned to exactly where they belong)	
Pride in accomplishments	Shows pride in accomplishments—"I did it!" or "Did it myself!"	No pride in accomplishments
Making of choices	• Easily distracted if too many choices provided • Toward end of period, can choose from an increased number of options of activities and materials	Still distracted by choices at end of this period
Gender identity	Gender identity is established around 1½ years, but child may not realize that he or she will always be a girl or boy	Lack of gender identity

PLAY

Toddlers' play is rich in symbolic actions; they will often use one object to represent another. As toddlers learn to share, their play gradually changes. Toward the end of this period, they start to interact more with other children and start to share ideas and toys.

TABLE 7.7 Play—2–3 Years

TYPE OF PLAY	DESCRIPTION	✳ DEVELOPMENTAL ALERT
Solitary	Solitary play in all activities but with some parallel play	Little parallel play observed
Symbolic/parallel	Evident in most learning areas (e.g., uses a twig to represent a boat during water play)	Limited symbolic play
Associative	Near the end of this period, plays beside others, sharing ideas and materials (**associative play**) but often plays independently also	

associative play
shares ideas and materials but continues to engage in solitary play

TABLE 7.8 Play with Materials—2–3 Years (Free Sensory Exploration Phase)

TYPE OF PLAY	DESCRIPTION	✳ DEVELOPMENTAL ALERT
Water	Explores and experiments with the sensation of water (e.g., feeling bubbles, splashing, moving objects in water, catching raindrops) (Crowther, 2003) (Photo 7.7)	
Sand	• Interested in the feel of sand, may even taste it • Still enjoys filling and dumping activities, plus burying objects	

Table 7.8 continues on next page

TABLE 7.8 Play with Materials—2–3 Years (Free Sensory Exploration Phase)

TYPE OF PLAY	DESCRIPTION	✳ DEVELOPMENTAL ALERT
Music	• Listens to music, moves rhythmically, and imitates others' movements to music • Starts to sing simple songs • Uses rhythm instruments to "play along" with music or a song • Uses different body parts to mark a simple beat (e.g., clapping, stamping, jumping; may not be able to keep the beat)	No participation in musical activities
Blocks	Rows and towers: Stacks blocks vertically or horizontally	Limited block play
Prop-dependent dramatic play	Available objects dictate the type of dramatic play that occurs (e.g., using construction vehicles in the sand may lead to digging, road-making, driving activities)	Limited dramatic play

PHOTO 7.7 By feeling bubbles, the toddler explores the sensation of water.

TOILETING

Some children, but not all, may complete toilet training during their second year.

✳ **DEVELOPMENTAL ALERTS**
- **Does not have regular dry periods**
- **Regularly has more than two bowel movements daily**

SELF-HELP SKILLS

Self-help skills continue to expand and become refined. By the end of this period, most toddlers:

- Wash own hands appropriately, with reminders.
- Brush own teeth.
- Become more independent in dressing themselves, needing help only with starting zippers, doing up buttons, or fastening shoes.
- Eat and drink independently.
- Put away toys when activity is completed but may need a reminder.

TOOLS FOR OBSERVING—TWO TO THREE YEARS

Blank versions of the observation charts in this section can be downloaded for your use from Nelson's Resource Centre for Early Childhood Education at www.ece.nelson.com.

SAMPLE 1
Manipulation Activities

Recording details of the child's manipulation activities will help to identify:
- Skill levels achieved.
- Emerging and waning interests.
- Materials needed to expand or maintain interests.
- Activities and materials to help in transferring skills to other settings (e.g., learning to pour water in the water centre can lead to pouring milk or juice at the snack table).

Manipulation Activities—2–3 Years

Name: Rashawne

MANIPULATION ACTIVITY	DESCRIPTION	DATE
Beading	• Placed 5 beads of different sizes and shapes on a pipe cleaner • Placed 5 round beads on another pipe cleaner • Ran to show both to teacher: "I did it!"	Oct. 2
Dumping and filling	Used coloured toy gems to fill bucket, then poured gems onto large tray; repeated activity 5 times	Oct. 5

SAMPLE 2
Types of Play

The purpose of the chart below is to identify:
- Type of play used.
- Emerging and waning interests.
- Materials needed to expand or maintain interests (e.g., simple role-playing in the sandbox, driving cars through the sand, may be transferred to the block area, where cars might be driven on top of a row of blocks).

Types of Play—2–3 Years

Name: Keegan

TYPE OF PLAY	DESCRIPTION AND FREQUENCY	DATE
Solitary	• At water area and sand area, filling and dumping ‖ • Looked at picture book *Playing with Pets* | • At baby bath area, washed doll		Oct. 3
Parallel		
Observer		
Role-playing		
Prop-dependent dramatic play		
Symbolic		

SAMPLE 3
Evaluation of Interest Areas

The type of chart shown below can be used to:
- Identify interest levels and type of activities engaged in by an individual toddler.
- Assess the effectiveness of the organization of a child-care centre.

In the sample chart on the next page, role-playing obviously has not been an area that has attracted the toddlers, indicating the need for some adaptations. The list of interest areas can easily be expanded as required.

Evaluation of Interest Areas (Child-Care Centre: Toddlers 2–3 Years)

INTEREST AREA	DESCRIPTION AND FREQUENCY OF USE	DATE
Sensory play	• Water play with bubbles ‖‖ ‖‖ • Sand play (outside) with vehicles ‖‖	Oct. 1
Painting	• On easel ‖ • Finger-painting ‖‖ ‖‖ ‖‖ ‖‖	Oct. 1
Role-playing		
Block play	• Transporting blocks ‖‖ ‖‖ • Building towers ‖‖ ‖‖ ‖‖ • Making rows ‖‖	Oct. 1–2
Book area	• Solitary play ‖‖ • Requests to have story read ‖‖ ‖‖	Oct. 2
Manipulation activities	• Beading ‖ • Puzzles ‖‖ • Small blocks ‖‖ • Sorting toys ‖‖ ‖‖	Oct. 1–2
Outdoor gross motor play	• Riding toys ‖‖ • Climbing ‖‖ ‖‖ • Playing with balls ‖‖ • Balance beam ‖ • Painting/drawing ‖‖	Oct. 1–2

REFERENCES

Crowther, I. (2003). *Creating effective learning environments*. Scarborough, ON: Nelson Thomson Learning.

THE PRESCHOOL YEARS

Three to Five

INTRODUCTION

Some variations exist across Canada in the ages of preschool children, but most jurisdictions accept that children three to five years old fall into the preschool category. In some public school areas, children can attend junior kindergarten at age four and senior kindergarten at age five.

GROWTH PATTERNS OF PRESCHOOLERS

The preschooler's appearance has changed quite dramatically, compared with the early toddler years. Legs and trunk have become much longer, contributing to the slimmer appearance of the child. The head is now more proportionate to the rest of the body.

The preschooler's growth slows down in comparison with the previous rapid growth patterns. At age three, the average child weighs 14 kg and will gain 4.1 to 4.5 kg each year between three and five years, weighing an average of 17.3 kg at age five.

Changes in height also slow down between the ages of three and five, with an average gain of 6.4 cm during that period. At age three, the average preschooler is 94 cm tall and by age five is about 113 cm tall.

DEVELOPMENTAL AREAS

A child's centre of gravity becomes evenly distributed during this period. By the time children are five or six years old, the centre of gravity is below their naval. As a result, they are no longer top-heavy and can coordinate physical movements much more readily.

An explosion of language capabilities occurs in this age group, and as many as six to seven new words may be learned every day. This language growth is matched by another growth spurt in brain development. During this period, it is critical to support the preschooler's development with activities that stimulate all domains of development—social, emotional, physical, cognitive, and language.

Growth in the cognitive development of this age group is demonstrated by preschoolers' abilities to better understand other people's perspectives and by progressive utilization of materials in the environment to learn more about concepts related to such areas as math, science, reading, writing, and computers.

Preschoolers need to function in environments that respects each child's right to:

- Learn through active play.
- Interact with adults and peers in an atmosphere of respect and trust.
- Receive recognition of, and support to enhance, their emergent knowledge and skills.
- An environment rich in challenges, choices, and opportunities to solve problems individually and in groups.

APPLICATION STAGE

Children use skills and knowledge gained to interact with the materials and activities in their learning environment. Continued growth in understanding leads to increased ability to act in more abstract activities, such as reading and writing.

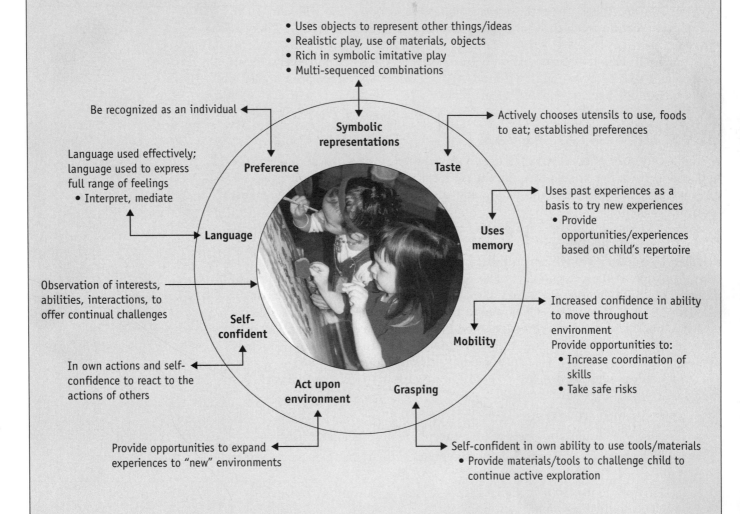

- Uses objects to represent other things/ideas
- Realistic play, use of materials, objects
- Rich in symbolic imitative play
- Multi-sequenced combinations

Be recognized as an individual

Language used effectively; language used to express full range of feelings
- Interpret, mediate

Symbolic representations

Preference

Taste

Actively chooses utensils to use, foods to eat; established preferences

Language

Uses past experiences as a basis to try new experiences
- Provide opportunities/experiences based on child's repertoire

Uses memory

Observation of interests, abilities, interactions, to offer continual challenges

Self-confident

Mobility

Increased confidence in ability to move throughout environment
Provide opportunities to:
- Increase coordination of skills
- Take safe risks

In own actions and self-confidence to react to the actions of others

Act upon environment

Grasping

Provide opportunities to expand experiences to "new" environments

Self-confident in own ability to use tools/materials
- Provide materials/tools to challenge child to continue active exploration

CHAPTER 8

Three to Four Years

"I had always enjoyed teaching toddlers because of their enthusiasm for learning. When I was told that I had the opportunity to follow my group of toddlers to the preschool program I was excited. I had not realized how much I would learn and how much I would enjoy this move. It was awesome to observe how children blossom when their background experiences are acknowledged and built upon."

INTRODUCTION

The three-year-old is a much more peaceful individual than the toddler. Three-year-olds are learning to better understand other people's perspectives and have therefore begun to learn to share. They are usually comfortable in their ability to be independent and enjoy interacting with other children to make choices, solve problems, and actively explore their environment.

PHYSICAL DEVELOPMENT

Three-year-olds usually have developed a number of gross and fine motor skills that increase their ability to learn and discover new things. Their motor skills have become more refined, leading to greater independence and increased ability to solve their own problems and make personal decisions.

TABLE 8.1	Gross Motor Development—3–4 Years	
SKILL	**DESCRIPTION**	**❋ DEVELOPMENTAL ALERT**
Balancing	• Can balance on one foot • Walks in a straight line • Walks a few steps on balance beam	• Poor balance • Often falls
Walking/running	• Walks with arms swinging • Runs more smoothly; better able to change direction and to stop	• Walks into obstacles • Unable to stop • Often falls
Climbing	• Climbs stairs using alternating feet; descends using one foot at time (Photo 8.1) • Climbs up climbing equipment but may have difficulty climbing down without help	• Continues to crawl up and down stairs • Avoids climbing apparatus
Jumping	• Jumps using both feet at the same time • Jumps over obstacles, leading with one foot • Jumps down from platforms, climbing equipment	• Limited jumping • Falls after jumping
Ball skills	• Throws ball overhand by extending the throwing arm and holding the body stiffly • Catches the ball by trapping it against body with arms and hands • Kicks ball while running; runs to catch up with the ball to kick it again	Continues to throw ball with two hands
Using riding toys	• Pedals on tricycle or other pedalled riding toys • Steers riding toys	Continues to push with feet to propel tricycle

PHOTO 8.1 Preschoolers climb stairs and ladders using alternating feet.

TABLE 8.2	**Fine Motor Development—3–4 Years**	
SKILL	**DESCRIPTION**	✳ **DEVELOPMENTAL ALERT**
Manipulation	• Cuts paper with scissors (Photo 8.2) • Controls crayons and markers to make vertical, horizontal, and circular strokes • Begins to use **tripod grasp** (holding a writing tool with two fingers and the thumb) (Photo 8.3) • May show hand dominance for some activities	• Difficulty manipulating scissors, markers, crayons • Use of palmar grasp
Artwork	*Controlled scribbling: 3 years* • More scribbles made in each drawing • Lines go in various directions • More loops and swirls appear • Pays more attention to where scribble is placed on paper—at the top, at the bottom, all over *Named scribbling: 3½–4 years* • Spends more time making marks • Names scribbles, but names may change during process • Relates scribbles to things in environment	• Scribbles disordered and random • Scribbles not named

tripod grasp
using two fingers and the thumb to hold a writing tool

Table 8.2 continues on next page

PHOTO 8.2 Increased fine motor dexterity is demonstrated by the ability to use scissors to cut paper.

TABLE 8.2	**Fine Motor Development—3–4 Years**	
SKILL	**DESCRIPTION**	**✳ DEVELOPMENTAL ALERT**
Artwork	• Holds tools with fingers (start of tripod grasp) • Uses greater variety of line shapes and directions • Places scribbles more intentionally • Wants to fill empty spaces (Crowther, 2003, p. 200) (Photo 8.4)	
Eye-hand coordination	• Engages in carpentry activities—hits nail on head • Pours with less spilling	Difficulty hitting where aimed or when pouring

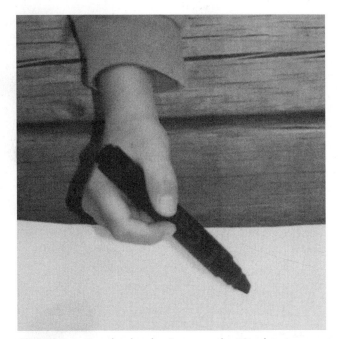

PHOTO 8.3 Preschoolers begin to use the tripod grasp.

PHOTO 8.4 Preschoolers demonstrate more intentional placement of scribbles and a desire to fill empty spaces on the sheet. In addition, they often name their artwork—Jenna named her drawing "A Monster."

SLEEP PATTERNS

Between three and four years of age, preschoolers:

- Sleep an average of 11 hours at night.
- May no longer need a nap during the day but should have a quiet time.
- May start to dream and may have nightmares that cause them to wake up.
- Are able to manage sleep-time routines independently.

BRAIN DEVELOPMENT

By the age of three, 1000 trillion connections have been formed in the preschooler's brain—twice as many as in an adult's brain. A spurt in brain growth coincides with increased language development.

EATING

At this stage, preschoolers:

- Serve themselves food, eat and drink independently, and pour their own drinks.
- May dislike cooked vegetables.

COGNITIVE DEVELOPMENT

As children gain increased control over their motor skills, they also increase their cognitive skills. Increased motor ability provides the opportunity for active exploration, and so children learn more about the world around them, as well as the concepts of function, size, colour, and shape.

TABLE 8.3	Cognitive Development—3–4 Years	
SKILL	**DESCRIPTION**	**✳ DEVELOPMENTAL ALERT**
Symbolic function	Selection of objects to represent other objects in pretend play not dependent on shape of an object (e.g., might use a square block to represent a cup)	Limited symbolic function
Visual perception	Can be fooled by the appearance of an object (e.g., might try to eat plastic fruit)	
Centration	Focuses on only one aspect of a problem (**centration**) (e.g., might say that a tall, skinny glass holds more than a short, fat glass, even though the opposite is true)	
Sorting	Sorts objects based on one characteristic (e.g., shape, colour, or size), but is easily distracted (e.g., may start sorting plastic bears by colour [red] but then switch to sorting by size when a large red bear is encountered; for example, sorts 6 red bears, the last one is a large red bear, and so starts sorting large blue bears)	Limited sorting ability

centration
focusing on only one aspect of a problem

Table 8.3 continues on next page

TABLE 8.3	Cognitive Development—3–4 Years	
SKILL	**DESCRIPTION**	**✳ DEVELOPMENTAL ALERT**
Concept development	• *Size:* Differentiates between large and small sizes • *Quantity:* Identifies when one set of items contains more than another (Photo 8.5) • *Time:* Expresses an understanding of time duration ("Sleep all night," "Play for a long time") • *Colour:* Starts to name colours • *Shapes:* Correctly identifies geometric shapes	Understanding of concepts not demonstrated
Counting	• **Rote counts** to 5 but may easily become confused and mix up numbers (e.g., 1, 2, 4, 3, 5) • Cannot say correctly how many items are involved	Does not rote count
Problem-solving	Uses materials to help solve problems (e.g., finds a different brush to make wider lines, makes sand a little wetter to form moulds)	Limited ability to solve problems

rote count
counting by memory without understanding the meaning of the numbers

PHOTO 8.5 Preschoolers' developing sense of quantity allows them to identify when one set of items contains more than another.

COMMUNICATION

Language skills develop at a tremendous rate, but three-year-olds need much repetition of new words used in context to be able to remember, pronounce, and use these words. Children in this age group also learn to understand and use symbolized language in other forms by:

- Associating words to words in print, such as in books; their own names on hooks; labels on items in storage containers or on storage shelves (e.g., art supplies, a shelf of sand toys).

- Listening to stories or the recounting of events by adults or peers, stories on audiotapes.

- Looking at pictures and photographs and noting details.

Children of this age can form letters and words on paper and recognize some words, such as their own names and the names of pets, foods, and toys.

TABLE 8.4 Language Development—3–4 Years

SKILL	DESCRIPTION	✳ DEVELOPMENTAL ALERT
Language usage	• Uses 3–4 words in simple sentences ("Daddy is at work") • Uses words to compare (e.g., more, longer, faster) • Repeats simple rhymes or fingerplays • Sings simple songs • Asks many questions • Talks about things that are not in the immediate vicinity ("My cat's black. She's at home") • Describes actions, events, feelings ("Cory is sad") • Maintains conversations by adding comments to what someone said ("It's a *red* ball"), asking questions about what has been heard ("Why did she do that?"), making suggestions ("Let's build a castle"), or answering questions appropriately • Uses descriptive words (e.g., big, red ball) • Uses language to describe what he or she is doing or seeing (e.g., in pretend play, "I am making coffee") • Listens to stories for 10 or more minutes • Makes relevant comments about stories heard • Identifies words that sound alike (e.g., ball and fall, toy and boy) • Tells stories or pretends to read to peers	• Points or uses gestures to communicate • Single-word usage
Grammar	• Utilizes plurals (e.g., apples, oranges, but may overextend by still saying "feets") • Puts endings on verbs (e.g., "-ing") • Uses negatives ("No more milk")	Plurals and verb endings not used
Vocabulary size	On average, 300–1000 words	

PERSONAL/SOCIAL DEVELOPMENT

Preschoolers are much calmer than toddlers and take a greater interest in their peers. They are more likely to share materials and ideas, thus becoming more involved with others and in group activities.

TABLE 8.5 Personal/Social Development—3–4 Years

SKILL	DESCRIPTION	✳ DEVELOPMENTAL ALERT
Emotional control	• Takes turns, but not consistently • Understands basic emotions and starts to use words to indicate feelings ("Sarah is happy") • Shows affection to younger children • Shows concern or affection for hurt child • Is usually friendly	• Erratic emotional outbursts • Difficulty in expressing emotions • Hard to comfort

Table 8.5 continues on next page

TABLE 8.5 Personal/Social Development—3–4 Years

SKILL	DESCRIPTION	✳ DEVELOPMENTAL ALERT
Emotional control	• Defends own rights ("I had it first") • May act aggressively (yelling, grabbing, hitting) if toy is taken or activity is disturbed by others	
Peer interaction	• Participates with peers in activities such as simple games or moving to music • Shares, but not consistently • May observe others before joining play	Limited interaction with peers
Pride in accomplishment	• Demonstrates enjoyment of having efforts recognized (e.g., artwork put on display) • Expresses pride ("I did it") (Photo 8.6)	No pride shown in personal efforts
Making choices	• Chooses from a wide variety of activities and materials • Still distracted by activities of peers	Continually distracted
Gender identity	States own gender correctly, but still has no concept that this gender will always be the same	Does not identify own gender

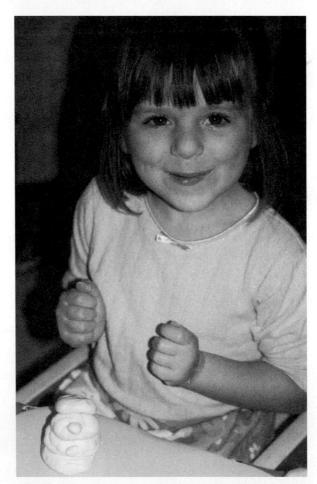

PHOTO 8.6 Preschoolers express pride in their accomplishments.

PLAY

Three-year-olds' play increasingly involves their peers. Children learn to negotiate with each other, make decisions about their learning, and become increasingly more creative and imaginative in their play activities.

TABLE 8.6	Play—3–4 Years	
TYPE OF PLAY	**DESCRIPTION**	**✹ DEVELOPMENTAL ALERT**
Observer	Observes before deciding to participate	
Solitary	• Plays alone by choice on occasion • Verbally expresses need to be alone	
Parallel	• May occur in all types of play (e.g., water, sand, art)	Solitary play only
Associative	• At the end of the third year, may start to share ideas and materials, but continues to engage in solitary play	
Constructive	• Starts to use objects and materials to express ideas or create structures (e.g., builds a field for farm animals) (**constructive play**) (Crowther, 2003) (Photo 8.7)	
Dramatic	• Acts out familiar roles (e.g., those of family members or of familiar people, such as doctors) • Interacts with peers in role-playing • Demonstrates feelings and personalities of individuals imitated • May tell others what he or she is going to do or whom he or she is playing ("I am a doctor") • May create an imaginary playmate	Limited dramatic play observed

constructive play
use of objects and materials to express ideas or create structures

PHOTO 8.7 In constructive play, children use objects and materials to express ideas and create structures.

TABLE 8.7   Play with Materials—3–4 Years

TYPE OF PLAY	DESCRIPTION	✳ DEVELOPMENTAL ALERT
Block	• Builds enclosures that may be labelled as rooms or fenced-in areas • Builds bridges and may drive vehicles under the bridges • Begins to name the structures (e.g., my house, a highway)	Limited block play other than carrying blocks around
Water	• Experiments to make connections (e.g., drops things into water to determine whether they sink or float) • Creates mixtures (e.g., water and art paint) • Imitates functional uses (e.g., washing clothes, dishes, or "babies") • Empties and fills containers • Recognizes water in the environment (rain, fog, snow, ice) (Crowther, 2003, p. 87)	Water used as a sensory experience only
Sand	• Experiments and makes connections (e.g., filling and dumping aid in understanding the concepts of weight, volume) • Constructs structures and names them • Understands the difference between wet and dry sand and how to use each	Lack of experimentation or building of structures
Music	• Experiments with instruments to create different sounds, volumes (Photo 8.8) • Keeps a steady beat when using rhythm instruments	Lack of experimenting with instruments

TOILETING

During this period, most children:

- are toilet trained, but may still need diapers at night.
- can independently use the toilet, but need reminders of appropriate routines.

INDEPENDENCE

In the three- to four-year period, most preschoolers are:

- More independent in carrying out self-care routines, although reminders may still be necessary.
- Able to dress self, but may need help with more difficult clothing (e.g., snowsuits) and starting zippers.
- Able to serve and feed self without assistance.

TOOLS FOR OBSERVING—THREE TO FOUR YEARS

Blank versions of the observation charts in this section can be downloaded for your use from Nelson's Resource Centre for Early Childhood Education at www.ece. nelson.com.

PHOTO 8.8 Preschoolers create different sounds and volume by experimenting with instruments.

SAMPLE 1
Types of Scribbles Made

The chart below enables you to identify:
- Variety of scribbles made.
- Additional materials to encourage more artwork.
- Milestones.

As shown in the chart below, a record should be kept of the types of lines and colours used, as well as placement of the scribble on the page.

Types of Scribbles—3–4 Years

Name: Jamie

TYPE OF SCRIBBLE	DESCRIPTION	DATE
Lines	Vertical, horizontal, straight and curved overlapped scribbles	Oct. 5
Colours	Red and blue crayons	
Placement	Filled whole page	

SAMPLE 2
Colour Recognition

In the chart below:
- Colours can be added as the child recognizes them.
- Additional columns can be added for insertion of comments related to various activities in which the colour was involved.

Colour Recognition—3–4 Years

Name: Jordan

COLOUR	MATCHING	SORTING	NAMING COLOURS	DATE
Red	• Identified that red bear was the same colour as own shirt • Confused red and orange	Strung all red beads	"Red bear"	Oct. 5

SAMPLE 3
Shape Recognition

The chart provided here can be used in the same manner as the colour recognition chart.

Shape Recognition—3–4 Years

Name: Yasmine

SHAPE	MATCHING	SORTING	LABELLING	DATE
Vehicles		Sorted cars from trucks	Accurate: Camero, dump truck, cement truck	Oct. 6
Geometric	Triangles, circles, rectangles, squares		Circle, triangle	Oct. 12

SAMPLE 4
Size Recognition

This chart can be used in the same manner as the colour recognition chart.

Size Recognition—3–4 Years

Name: Joyce

SIZE	MATCHING	SORTING	LABELLING	DATE
Big and small		Big bears and little bears of various colours (red, yellow, green, blue)	Correct labels for size and colours (big red bear, little green bear)	Oct. 6

REFERENCES

Crowther, I. (2003). *Creating effective learning environments*. Scarborough, ON: Nelson Thomson Learning.

CHAPTER 9

Four Years

"I really enjoy my four-year-old daughter Laura. She has become a real companion. She loves to help me with all the things I do. She has become very independent. Laura gets up by herself and rarely forgets the normal routines such as brushing her teeth. She has become very thoughtful. The other day she helped her dad make coffee in the morning. She ran out to the garden to get a flower. Then she brought coffee and the flower in a vase to me in bed. She is so enthusiastic about learning everything. She continually explores her environment to gain more understanding about the things around her. I just love this age."

INTRODUCTION

Four-year-olds have become much more independent. They are starting to form their own ideas and may debate these with their peers. They actively explore the environment with self-confidence and enthusiasm. They also are very communicative, using their increased language skills to talk about everything—continually.

PHYSICAL DEVELOPMENT

Children in this age group gain increased fine motor control dexterity, which makes tasks such as threading beads simpler and more efficient than previously. They may start to show hand dominance for some activities, such as cutting only with the right hand.

TABLE 9.1	Gross Motor Development—4 Years	
SKILL	**DESCRIPTION**	✳ **DEVELOPMENTAL ALERT**
Balancing	• Walks on a circular line • Walks across a balance beam	Difficulty balancing
Walking/running	• Runs with increased speed and agility (primarily gallops) • Navigates sharp corners while running • Stops easily • Skips with one foot	• Falls frequently • Stumbles into or over obstacles
Climbing	• Uses alternating feet to ascend and descend stairs • Climbs up and down all parts of climbing equipment (ladders, stairs, ropes, poles) • Uses natural outdoor environment to climb (e.g., trees, fences, rocks)	Climbs stairs one foot at a time
Jumping	• By about 4½, swings arms and leans forward to jump ahead in a two-footed take-off • Leads with one foot when jumping over obstacles • Jumps down from higher obstacles, climbers, platforms • Hops on one foot for a short time	• Does not attempt to jump • Falls frequently when jumping
Ball play	• Throws ball overhand; steps forward with body still fairly stiff but with some rotation, pulls back arm, and releases ball • Focuses on the ball to catch it and uses just the hands to catch the ball • Has better control when kicking a ball; ball stays close to foot as the child kicks and runs after it	Limited ball activity
Riding toys	• Pedals with increased speed and control around obstacles • Steers around corners • Avoids "traffic" and other obstacles	Continues to propel self on riding toys by pushing with feet

TABLE 9.1	**Gross Motor Development—4 Years** *(continued)*	
SKILL	**DESCRIPTION**	✳ **DEVELOPMENTAL ALERT**
Eye–hand coordination	• Shows more accuracy in hitting nails on the head and pegs into a pegboard (Photo 9.1) • Threads various types of wooden beads onto gimp • Sews around outside of sewing card (Photo 9.2)	• Misses head of nail or peg consistently • Does not bead or sew

TABLE 9.2	**Fine Motor Development—4 Years**	
SKILL	**DESCRIPTION**	✳ **DEVELOPMENTAL ALERT**
Manipulation	• Cuts out simple shapes such as circles and squares • Reproduces simple shapes such as circles and rectangles • Starts to reproduce some letters, although the letters may be hard to recognize • May reproduce own name or part of name • Has a refined tripod grasp	• No attempt to reproduce shapes or letters • Continued use of palmar grasp
Artwork	• Scribbles take on recognizable forms (e.g., geometric shapes) • Places scribbles randomly on the page; sizes of scribbles vary • Forms combinations of shapes (e.g., triangles and rectangles together) • Starts to draw human figures—usually stick figures with heads, arms, and legs, although legs might emerge from the head, and not all parts of head, arms, and feet are present • May draw several unrelated objects on the same page (Photo 9.3) • Uses colour randomly • Draws only front view of objects (Crowther, 2003, p. 200)	• Scribbles disordered and random • Scribbles not named

SLEEP PATTERNS

During a child's fourth year:

- A regular sleep pattern is usually established.
- The child may or may not need an afternoon nap.
- Afternoon sleep may interfere with regular night-time sleep patterns.
- Some children may develop a fear of the dark and may need a light left on.

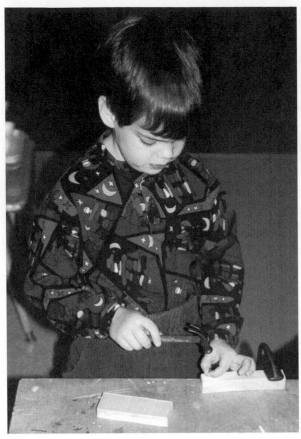

PHOTO 9.1 Hitting nails and pegs with greater accuracy is one of the emergent skills of four-year-olds.

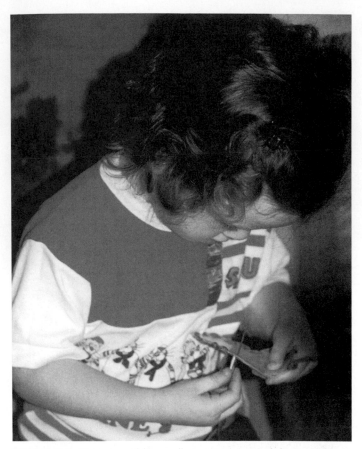

PHOTO 9.2 Four-year-olds usually can sew around the outside of a sewing card.

PHOTO 9.3 Several unrelated objects may be drawn on one page.

BRAIN DEVELOPMENT

Critical social and cognitive skills are developed during the child's fourth year of life, resulting in increased neural connections. Integration of sensory input through a number of neural pathways provides greater efficiency. For example, information received from the tactile sense (picking up a small ball) becomes integrated with gross motor movement (throwing the ball), an understanding of the actions (picking up and throwing), and the name of item used (ball) (McCain & Mustard, 1999).

EATING

By this age, children:

- Have definite food likes and dislikes.
- Will refuse to eat foods that are not liked.
- Enjoy helping with food preparation.
- Enjoy the social aspects of mealtime and may have to be reminded to eat.

COGNITIVE DEVELOPMENT

At this age, children continue to learn how items function, how to use items, and to gain familiarity with using items in a variety of ways. Through active exploration, children gain relevant experiences to transfer knowledge from situation to situation. For example, a ball may be used to hit, to throw, to kick, or to roll, depending on the activity.

TABLE 9.3	Cognitive Development—4 Years	
SKILL	**DESCRIPTION**	**❊ DEVELOPMENTAL ALERT**
Symbolic function	Selection of one object to represent another in pretend play is dependent on the use of both objects—the more familiar a child is with an object's use, the less likely it is that it will be used inappropriately (e.g., would not use a bat to represent a fishing rod)	Symbolic function reserved to gestures and using similarly shaped objects
Visual perception	Can still be fooled by the appearance of objects (e.g., plastic or wax fruit); might verbalize that it is pretend fruit but still try to eat it	
Centration	Still focuses on only one aspect of a problem (e.g., will say a tall, skinny glass [less quantity] holds more than a short, fat glass [more quantity] because the tall glass looks "bigger" [i.e., taller], even if the child compares the amount by pouring each glass's contents into other identical containers)	
Sorting	• Starts to sort by colour • Is less likely to be distracted while sorting (e.g., can progress through sorting pink dogs, to red dogs, to light pink cats, to dark pink dogs, to red birds) (Photo 9.4)	Does not recognize similarities and differences in colour

Table 9.3 continues on next page

TABLE 9.3	Cognitive Development—4 Years	
SKILL	**DESCRIPTION**	✳ **DEVELOPMENTAL ALERT**
Concept development	• *Size:* Stacks nesting cups or cubes by trial and error; may miss some in the stacking process; can identify objects as "biggest," "tallest," etc. • *Quantity:* Understands concept of "more," "most," etc. • *Time:* Understands daily sequence of routines (e.g., getting up in the morning, brushing teeth, getting dressed, having breakfast, etc.) • *Differences:* Identifies what is missing from a picture or puzzle • *Similarities:* Matches things that are the same	Limited understanding of these concepts
Counting	May rote count to 20, but may miss numbers or insert incorrect numbers	Difficulty rote counting to 10

PHOTO 9.4 Four-year-olds are less likely to be distracted in their sorting.

COMMUNICATION

Communication skills continue to expand rapidly during the fourth year. The children's sense of humour is evolving, and they delight in creating nonsense words. The ability to differentiate words that are similar also provides creative opportunities to form silly rhymes and songs.

TABLE 9.4 Language Development—4 Years

SKILL	DESCRIPTION	✳ DEVELOPMENTAL ALERT
Language usage	• Creates more complex sentences ("I went to the store with Mom and we bought ice cream)" • Asks and answers questions involving who, what, why • Talks at length about things, events, or people not in the immediate vicinity • Changes manner of speaking depending on the audience (e.g., simplifies language to speak to younger children) • Changes voice tone during role-playing to imitate different individuals • Recites an increasing number of simple nursery rhymes • Expands repertoire of simple songs sung • States full name	• Uses only phrases or simple sentences • Unable to recite or sing simple rhymes or songs • Talks only about things in the immediate vicinity
Grammar	• Uses prepositions (e.g., on, in, under) • Uses possessive pronouns and nouns (e.g., hers, his, theirs, Mommy's, pony's) • Uses the past tense ("I went to visit my grandmother in Vancouver)" • May still use overextensions ("I hurted myself")	• Prepositions, possessive terms, and plurals not used • Talks only about the present • Does not use spatial terms correctly
Reading	• May recognize some words (e.g., own name, name of favourite cereal) • May be able to read simple books • Names up to 20 letters of alphabet	Does not initiate looking at books
Writing	• Prints own name (Photo 9.5) • Copies words from labels around the room • May **scribble write** (use scribbling with the intent to create a written message) • Dictates stories	No evidence of using scribbles with intent to write

scribble write
using scribbling with the intent to create a written message

PERSONAL/SOCIAL DEVELOPMENT

Four-year-olds are usually outgoing, friendly individuals. They are very independent, can choose what they want to do from a variety of options, and are starting to solve interpersonal problems with guidance from adults.

Dealing with frustration is difficult for four-year-olds, and they may become very upset if they cannot find the toy they want or if they cannot accomplish what they want to do, such as creating a mould in the sand. Rapid mood changes from laughter to tears are a possible result. At this age, children may be able to voice what the problem is but are not always aware of why they are upset.

PHOTO 9.5 Four-year-olds often can print their own names.

TABLE 9.5	Personal/Social Development—4 Years	
SKILL	**DESCRIPTION**	✳ **DEVELOPMENTAL ALERT**
Emotional control	• Experiences sudden mood swings; may not know why • Has difficulty dealing with frustration • May sulk if left out of activity • Shares ideas and materials, but not consistently	Difficult to settle after mood swings or frustrating experiences
Peer interaction	• Forms friendships • May call peers names or disown a friend because of a disagreement • May exclude some peers from play • May boast about personal accomplishments and exaggerate abilities ("I can jump the highest. I jumped down from our roof.") • May use humour inappropriately (e.g., use "bathroom talk" while eating)	Ignores peers

TABLE 9.5 Personal/Social Development—4 Years *(continued)*

SKILL	DESCRIPTION	✳ DEVELOPMENTAL ALERT
Pride in accomplishments	• Asks to have efforts displayed • Asks adults and peers for approval of accomplishments	Does not show pride in accomplishments
Making choices	• Makes appropriate choices from a wide range of materials and activities • May interact with peers to make group decisions	Difficulty making choices

PLAY

Play continues to evolve as children become less egocentric and begin to share ideas and materials.

TABLE 9.6 Play—4 Years

TYPE OF PLAY	DESCRIPTION	✳ DEVELOPMENTAL ALERT
Solitary, parallel, observer	Continues solitary, parallel, and observer play by choice or as dictated by available materials (e.g., completing a painting may be a solitary activity)	Predominance of observer or solitary play
Associative	Firmly established—usually readily shares ideas and materials	
Constructive	Increasingly engages in constructive play with blocks, sand, dough, or clay, manipulates toys; does three-dimensional art, sewing, carpentry (Photo 9.6)	Limited constructive play
Dramatic	• Repeats favourite dramatic play • Dramatic play may extend over longer periods of time, including several days • Takes on roles of nonfamiliar people (e.g., firefighters, police officers) • May create adventure play along with role-play of imaginary people (e.g., superheroes, princesses, monsters); understands this is pretend play • Uses more symbolic representations to support play • Re-enacts experiences (e.g., zoo visit)	Dramatic play limited to symbolic activity

TABLE 9.7	Play with Materials—4 Years	
TYPE OF PLAY	**DESCRIPTION**	**✳ DEVELOPMENTAL ALERT**
Block	• Builds combinations of rows, towers, enclosures, bridges • Uses blocks as accessories for role-playing and dramatic play activities • May create patterns (e.g., a vertical enclosure of long rectangular blocks with a vertical block at each corner) • Builds alone or with others	Block play limited to stacking activities
Water	• Experiments to make connections (e.g., drops things into water to determine whether they sink or float) and comparisons (e.g., container is light when empty, heavy when full) • Creates mixtures of water and other materials for pretend play (e.g., as pretend food for "babies") (Photo 9.7) • Brings ice and snow inside to watch them melt	Water activities limited to sensory exploration
Sand	Creates and names structures of sand	Sand activities limited to sensory exploration
Musical activities	• Reproduces sounds, tones, and rhythmic patterns using instruments • Demonstrates an understanding of tempo, volume, and pitch in playing instruments • Coordinates two movements—marching and keeping a steady beat	• Cannot keep a beat • Cannot identify changes in pitch

INDEPENDENCE

Four-year-olds are quite independent in their self-care routines (e.g., toileting, eating) and in dressing themselves, but they may need help with some clothing, such as snowsuits.

TOOLS FOR OBSERVING—FOUR YEARS

Blank versions of the observation charts in this section can be downloaded for your use from Nelson's Resource Centre for Early Childhood Education at www.ece.nelson.com.

SAMPLE 1
Musical Activities

The purpose of the chart below is to identify:
- Musical milestones.
- Musical interests.
- New materials and experiences based on interests and abilities of the child.

Musical Activities—4 Years

Name: Billy

SKILL	DESCRIPTION	DATE
Beat	Marched and kept time to *Twinkle, Twinkle, Little Star*	Oct. 3
Pitch	As he listened to the piano play, he raised his hands and lowered them as the pitch rose and fell	Oct. 7
Volume	Matched, according to volume, containers that when shaken made different sounds—loud, soft, no sound	Oct. 10
Imitation	• Used bongo drum to copy beat set by adult (ta-ta-tee-tee-ta)	Oct. 4
	• Initiated a beat on bongo drum (tee-tee-tee-tee-ta-ta) and asked adult to copy it	Oct. 5

Sample 2
Cutting Skills

The cutting skills chart identifies:
- Skill levels.
- Appropriate experiences and materials to be provided.

Cutting Skills—4 Years

Name:

SKILL	DESCRIPTION	DATE
Experiments (snips, tears)		
Cuts across paper		
Cuts on the line		
Cuts out shapes		

Sample 3
Writing

Charting development of the child's writing skills helps to identify:
- Emergent writing skills that can be encouraged.
- Relevant experiences and materials to provide.
- Child's interests.

Writing—4 Years

Name: Jonathan

SKILL	DESCRIPTION	DATE
Scribbles with intent		
Forms letters		
Prints name	• Started at top right corner and when he ran out of room, printed letters going down right-hand side • Reversed "J"	Nov. 1
Forms words	• Colour words—red, blue • Copied the names purple, orange, and green from a colour chart	Nov. 5

REFERENCES

Crowther, I. (2003). *Creating effective learning environments*. Scarborough, ON: Nelson Thomson Learning.

McCain, M., & Mustard, F. (1999). *Early years study: Final report*. Toronto, ON: Publications Ontario.

CHAPTER 10

Five Years

The age of five often marks the first year of school in the elementary school system, meaning that there is a transition from early childhood to early primary years. The resultant increased expectations often cause the child to swing from dependency—wanting a hug and a kiss—to independence—not wanting to be hugged or kissed in front of their friends.

INTRODUCTION

Five-year-olds continue to learn by building on previous experiences, practising and refining their skills. They are more self-confident about their abilities and more independent in all areas, which could cause problems because they may not correctly assess potentially dangerous situations.

PHYSICAL DEVELOPMENT

Five-year-olds have greater control over their physical abilities. They constantly practise their emergent motor skills to gain greater mastery of them.

TABLE 10.1	Gross Motor Development—5 Years	
SKILL	**DESCRIPTION**	**✳ DEVELOPMENTAL ALERT**
Balance	• Moves across balance beam with increasingly better balance and more speed • Can balance on one foot for at least 10 seconds	Poor balance
Walking/ running	• Walks and runs more like an adult • Walks backward • Uses heel-to-toe gait • Skips with alternating feet • Shows increased control and speed in running	Limited increase in running and walking skills
Climbing	Climbs more like an adult	Limited climbing
Jumping	• Jumps over obstacles with both feet together • Can jump higher and farther • Jumps down from greater heights • Uses a skipping rope	Jumping not coordinated
Ball skills	• Steps forward to throw ball overhand; uses whole body and arm extension • Catches ball thrown from greater distances (at least 9.12 cm) • Kicks ball while running by keeping ball close to kicking foot • Kicks ball farther	• Lack of strength in throwing • Catches ball by extending arms and trapping ball against the body
Manipulation	• Cuts out preformed shapes, such as circles or squares • Reproduces many shapes in artwork (Photo 10.1) • Reproduces most letters; sometimes reverses letters • Reproduces own name • Colours inside lines	• No attempt to use scissors • No attempt to reproduce shapes or letters • Continued use of palmar grasp

PHOTO 10.1 Many different shapes may appear in five-year-olds' artwork.

TABLE 10.2	Fine Motor Development—5 Years	
SKILL	**DESCRIPTION**	✳ **DEVELOPMENTAL ALERT**
Manipulation	• Tripod grasp refined • Hand dominance established for most activities	
Artwork	• Scribbles take on recognizable forms • Reproduces increased number of recognizable geometric forms • Chooses sizes of elements in drawings more deliberately, although some sizes may not be realistic (e.g., depictions of family members may be larger than the house in a drawing). • Uses combinations of shapes to depict objects (e.g., a combination of triangles and rectangles may make up a house) • Adds additional body-part detail to drawings of human figures (e.g., fingers), but others may still be missing (neck, elbows) (Photo 10.2) • Starts to use colours selectively • Still draws only front views of objects (Crowther, 2003, p. 200)	• Disordered and random scribbles • Scribbles not named • No recognizable forms created
Eye–hand coordination	• Can attach two pieces of wood together with nails or screws • Threads long strings of beads, using beads of various sizes • Sews two pieces of material together (paper, plastic, fabric)	• Misses nail when hammering • Difficulty putting beads on gimp

PHOTO 10.2 Five-year-olds' depictions of human figures might still lack some body parts.

SLEEP PATTERNS

The five-year-old usually:

- Will get ready for bed independently and may begin to volunteer to go to bed when tired.
- No longer requires a nap during the day.
- Begins to have dreams and nightmares.
- Averages 10 hours sleep per night.

BRAIN DEVELOPMENT

Social and cognitive skills continue to develop during a child's fifth year, with resultant increased neural connections. Integration of sensory input through a number of neural pathways continues (McCain & Mustard, 1999).

EATING

The five-year-old is usually quite independent in eating routines and:

- Serves self and cleans up.
- Can prepare own breakfast (e.g., cereal or toast, milk, juice).
- Can prepare a sandwich for lunch (e.g., spreads toppings on bread, such as peanut butter, or adds meat or cheese and perhaps lettuce).

COGNITIVE DEVELOPMENT

Depending on background experiences and/or cultural values, some children may be capable of decentration earlier or later than others. **Decentration** is the ability to look at more than one aspect of a problem or situation at the same time; for example, children who have had experience in sorting objects will be able to create consistent patterns (red round bead, green round bead, red round bead, green round bead) without being distracted by other variables, such as different-coloured or different-shaped beads.

Children who are more dependent will find decentration more difficult. If an adult is always ready to help, the child does not need to think about the various aspects of an activity. For example, Shane was trying to put a puzzle together, and his mother handed him the correct puzzle piece. When he could not fit the piece in, she told him to turn it around. When that was not successful, she took it out of his hand and showed him how to do it. This type of situation creates dependence. If Shane does not gain experience by solving his own problems, he will not develop the ability to view problems and situations from different perspectives.

decentration
ability to look at more than one aspect of a problem or situation at the same time

TABLE 10.3	Cognitive Development—5 Years	
SKILL	**DESCRIPTION**	**✳ DEVELOPMENTAL ALERT**
Symbolic function	Chooses one object to represent another in pretend play based on availability of objects rather than similarity of use	Dependent on props and substitutions that look similar to the represented item
Visual perception	No longer fooled by the appearance of objects, such as wax or plastic fruit	
Centration	Focuses on more than one aspect of a problem or situation (decentration) (e.g., will figure out whether a tall, skinny glass holds more than a short, fat glass by pouring the water from one glass into the other)	
Sorting	• May start to sort familiar items by more than one characteristic by the beginning of the fifth year (e.g., will pick out apples from a mixture of familiar fruits and vegetables) • Can use two criteria to sort objects (e.g., using size and colour criteria, can sort all large, red objects from a variety of objects of different sizes and colours) • Sorts a variety of objects into groups that share a characteristic (e.g., separates into groups all vehicles, all farm animals) (Photo 10.3)	Continues to be distracted by other characteristics when sorting

Table 10.3 continues on next page

TABLE 10.3 Cognitive Development—5 Years

SKILL	DESCRIPTION	✳ DEVELOPMENTAL ALERT
Concept development	• *Size:* Can identify smallest and largest objects, shortest and longest objects • *Quantity:* Can identify "more" and "less" in both volume and number • *Seriation:* Arranges objects in order of size by trial-and-error method; identifies first, second, and last • *Time:* May be able to tell time by the hour (e.g., knows when it is time to be picked up: "When the little hand points to . . .") • *Numbers:* Identifies concept of "half" (e.g., half of an orange); puts two triangles together to form a square or rectangle • *Match:* Matches same size, same shape, same colour • *Money:* Names penny, nickel, dime, quarter • *Alphabet:* May name both uppercase and lowercase letters of the alphabet	Difficulty understanding or using these concepts
Counting	• Rote counts to 10 accurately • Rote counts to 20 (some children, to 100), but may miss numbers or use incorrect numbers	Limited rote counting

PHOTO 10.3 Five-year-olds can sort a variety of objects into groups that share a characteristic.

COMMUNICATION

Five-year-olds have become skilled communicators, with a vocabulary that has expanded to over 1500 words. They become adept at telling stories, jokes, and riddles, and enjoy talking on the telephone. Increased communicative abilities lead to establishing friendships and interacting in small or large group settings.

TABLE 10.4	Language Development—5 Years	
SKILL	**DESCRIPTION**	**✳ DEVELOPMENTAL ALERT**
Language usage	• Puts more than one sentence together to tell a story or relate an experience • Uses functional definitions (e.g. ropes twirl, kettles boil water) • States full address • States birth date • Takes simple telephone messages and relays them	• Uses short sentences only • Limited verbal interactions with peers
Grammar	• Uses verbs correctly—regular and irregular, past and present tense • Uses "would" and "could" correctly	Does not use verbs correctly
Reading	• Reads familiar words on cereal boxes, street signs, etc. • May read simple books • Names all letters of the alphabet	No evidence of reading ability
Writing	• Prints names of friends and family • Copies words from books, lists, labels posted around the classroom • May send notes to friends that usually are a combination of scribble writing and real words • Dictates stories (Photo 10.4)	Limited writing to express intent

PERSONAL/SOCIAL DEVELOPMENT

Five-year-olds are very interested in each other. Friendships continue to be formed, and children interact in group situations. Cooperation with peers and adults is a key development during this stage. Five-year olds follow directions and can be relied on to carry out specific tasks and activities.

TABLE 10.5	Personal Social Development—5 Years	
SKILL	**DESCRIPTION**	**✳ DEVELOPMENTAL ALERT**
Emotional control	• Fewer mood swings • Seeks adult reassurance and comfort in less obvious ways (e.g., plays close to the adult; continually looks at the adult from a distance) • Empathetic toward children or animals who have been hurt, showing concern and affection • Affectionate toward younger children	Continued mood swings

Table 10.5 continues on next page

TABLE 10.5 Personal Social Development—5 Years

SKIL	DESCRIPTION	❋ DEVELOPMENTAL ALERT
Peer interactions	• One or two "best" friends • Shares materials and ideas • Takes turns • Humour used to entertain peers and adults (e.g., tells jokes and riddles, imitates funny situations)	• Few friends • Finds it hard to relate positively to peers
Pride in accomplishments	Boasts about personal achievements	Limited pride in achievements

PLAY

Five-year-olds engage in a variety of play activities by choice. As children gain increased skill in negotiation, turn-taking, and sharing, they start to take part in more cooperative activities.

PHOTO 10.4 Five-year-olds can dictate stories.

TABLE 10.6   Play—5 Years

TYPE OF PLAY	DESCRIPTION	✳ DEVELOPMENTAL ALERT
Associative, solitary, parallel, observer	Associative, solitary, parallel, and observer play continue by choice or as dictated by materials or activities (e.g., completing a painting may be a solitary activity)	Predominance of solitary or observer play
Constructive	Constructive play is used to support role-playing, dramatic play, and group play	Limited constructive play
Cooperative	Chooses desired type of activity (e.g., building a zoo) and decides what materials are needed; assigns roles to build structures (e.g., one child builds fences, another child gathers animals, and a third child gathers materials to create trees and other plants); and assigns roles for continued play (e.g., the roles of a zookeeper or various animals and other people) (**cooperative play**) (Photo 10.5)	• Associative play predominates when with groups • Few instances of cooperative behaviour
Dramatic play and role-playing	• Communicates to identify common goals, plan play, and assign roles • Uses a variety of skills to enhance dramatic play (e.g., mime, creation of signs and props) • Negotiates with peers in small or larger groups • Extends play situation over time (e.g., for several days or even several weeks) • Expands dramatic theme using books and results of discussion	Limited role assignment or planning

cooperative play
two or more children work toward a common goal that includes sharing materials, ideas, and space, along with role designation

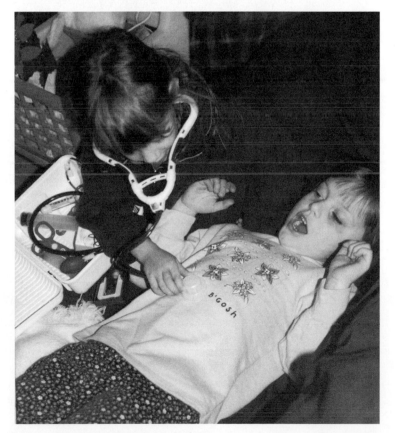

PHOTO 10.5 Planned cooperative play is often observed with five-year-olds.

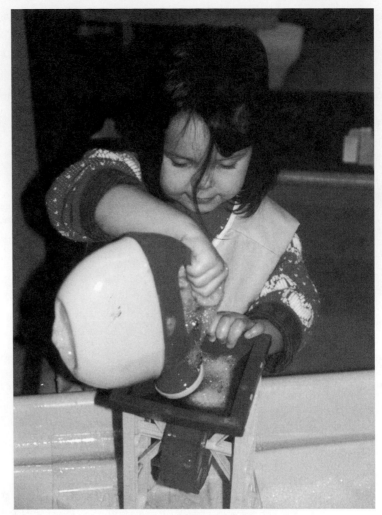

PHOTO 10.6 The water play of five-year-olds may involve directing the flow of water.

TABLE 10.7	**Play with Materials—5 Years**	
TYPE OF PLAY	**DESCRIPTION**	✳ **DEVELOPMENTAL ALERT**
Block	• Plans block play with others • Builds realistic structures and names structures • Adds more detail to structures (e.g., windows, doorways) • Uses structures to engage in dramatic play • Supports play by creating signs • Play extended over time	• Few recognizable structures created or named • Play confined to short periods of time
Water	• Increased experimentation (e.g., making floating items sink by adding objects to them, directing the flow of water toward objects to make them move at different speeds) (Photo 10.6)	Limited experimentation observed

TABLE 10.7	**Play with Materials—5 Years** *(continued)*	
TYPE OF PLAY	**DESCRIPTION**	**✳ DEVELOPMENTAL ALERT**
Music	• Recognizes simple songs from rhythm • Creates own songs • Creates own rhythms • Plays simple songs on piano or xylophone	Few creative musical efforts
Sand	• Increased constructive play in sand area • Elaborate structures built in collaboration with other children, often lasting over a long time period (days or weeks)	Limited constructive play observed

TOOLS FOR OBSERVING—FIVE YEARS

Blank versions of the observation charts in this section can be downloaded for your use from Nelson's Resource Centre for Early Childhood Education at www.ece.nelson.com.

SAMPLE 1
Constructive Play

Figure 10.1 is an example of how a child's constructive play development can be tracked, identifying:
- Types of structures made.
- Language used to identify structures.

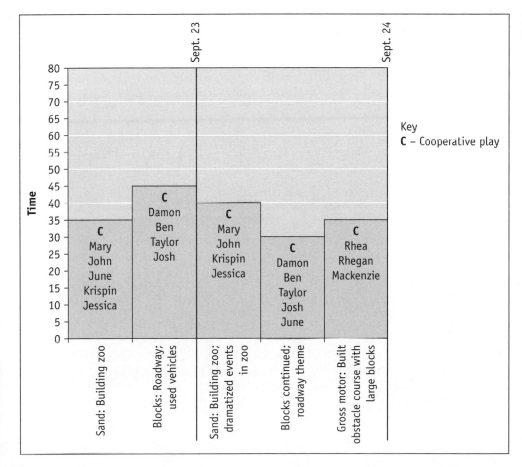

FIGURE 10.1 Constructive Play—5 Years

- Emergent or refined skills demonstrated.
- Materials used.
- Preferred interests.

SAMPLE 2
Block Play

Using a chart similar to the one below to record observations of a child's block play over time can identify the child's:
- Current interests.
- Attention span.
- Skills in certain situations (e.g., in cooperative play).
- Types of preferred dramatic play.

Recording the above can also help to identify materials and resources that could be provided to extend play activities. In the "Description" column, an account of the types of materials used and what has been accomplished could be inserted.

Block Play—5 Years

Name:

ACTIVITY	DESCRIPTION	DATE
Transporting blocks		
Rows and towers		
Enclosures and bridges		
Representational		

SAMPLE 3
Block Play

Figure 10.2 is an example of another way in which a child's block play can be recorded to assist in identifying:
- Types of structure made.
- Interests.
- Skill levels.
- Milestones reached in block play.
- Materials and resources to support and extend play.

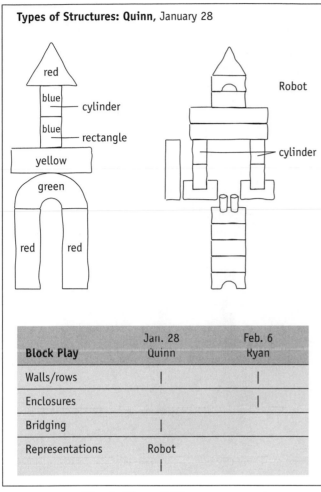

Types of Structures: Quinn, January 28

red
blue — cylinder
blue — rectangle
yellow
green
red   red

Robot
— cylinder

Block Play	Jan. 28 Quinn	Feb. 6 Ryan
Walls/rows	|	|
Enclosures		|
Bridging	|	
Representations	Robot |	

FIGURE 10.2 Block Play—5 Years

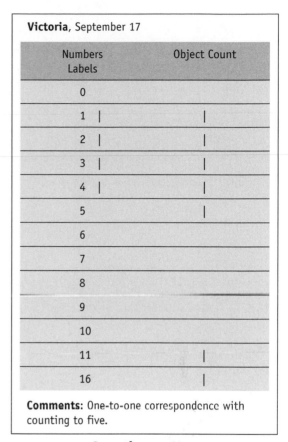

Victoria, September 17

Numbers Labels	Object Count
0	
1 |	|
2 |	|
3 |	|
4 |	|
5	|
6	
7	
8	
9	
10	
11	|
16	|

Comments: One-to-one correspondence with counting to five.

FIGURE 10.3 Counting—5 Years

Sample 4
Counting

W W W

Figure 10.3 is an example of a chart that can be used to help identify:
- Counting skill levels.
- Milestones reached in counting skills.
- Materials and resources to support and extend counting activities.

REFERENCES

Crowther, I. (2003). *Creating effective learning environments.* Scarborough, ON: Nelson Thomson Learning.

McCain, M., & Mustard, F. (1999). *Early years study: Final report.* Toronto, ON: Government of Ontario, Publications Ontario.

THE EARLY SCHOOL YEARS

Six to Eight

INTRODUCTION

The early school years (six to eight) are a period of steady physical growth and refinement of acquired skills and abilities. There are dramatic changes in children's cognitive abilities, such as the ability to read and write. They have gained self-control and interact within a variety of social settings.

Children of six are usually in school on a full-time basis and may also attend before- and after-school programs. These programs provide activities for children from the ages of 6 to 12 for whom other adult supervision is not available before and after school. In some areas, supervised lunch-hour programs are also provided.

GROWTH PATTERNS

At six years old, the differences in weight and height between boys and girls are minor; the average weight is 19.5 kg and the average height is 111.8 cm. Although it varies from child to child, girls and boys between the ages of six and eight gain about 2 to 3 kg per year and 5 to 7.5 cm of height per year. A significant amount of the weight gain is due to muscle growth, which leads to the development of greater strength and the ability to participate in a variety of sports and activities that require gross motor skills.

BRAIN DEVELOPMENT

Brain weight is equal to that of an adult by the age of six, and children have many more neural connections than are needed. To make the connections more efficient, a natural process called "pruning" takes place throughout the school years, and connections that have not been used begin to disappear. Those that have been used repeatedly remain.

DEVELOPMENT OF PERMANENT TEETH

Children may lose their first baby tooth at five, but this is most common for six-year-olds. All permanent teeth usually have erupted by 11 or 12 years of age, except for the two sets of molars.

INDEPENDENCE

Children between the ages of six and eight are usually fully independent in all their self-care routines. In addition, sets of rules for both home and school have been learned and are usually followed. Rules for home might require children to:

- Tell the family where they are going and when they will be home.
- Watch only approved types of television programs and play only certain video games.
- Follow established daily routines (e.g., mealtimes, bedtimes) and do assigned household chores.
- Show respect for others' privacy (e.g., for others' personal space and possessions).

The rules for school might require children to:

- Take responsibility for getting to school and completing assignments on time.
- Behave appropriately in class and in the schoolyard.

- Meet certain daily expectations for their academic schoolwork.
- Show respect for others' privacy.

FRIENDSHIPS

These are the years in which friendships are formed and maintained, and much of the children's social activity revolves around their friends. These friendships may change because these early relationships are often based on external factors such as physical attributes (appearance or strength, for example) or ability in sports.

PLAY

All forms of play continue to exist in the early school years. The type of play children engage in is usually dependent on individual choice, whether free play or imposed academic activities are involved, and the expectations imposed by adults or the environment. **Competitive play**—activities that have set rules and identify a winner or loser at the end of the play—gains prominence.

competitive play
activities that have imposed rules and identify a winner or loser at the end of the play

COMPETITION

In the early school years, children usually become more competitive and must learn to cope with competition in many areas, not just in play. For many children, competition means that they may never be considered "the best" and will need help in learning to cope with such disappointments. With the appropriate support, children can continue to develop a healthy self/ego.

Areas in which children in this age group will probably encounter competition include:

- Academic achievement (e.g., grades, spelling bees).
- Sports (e.g., trying out for school teams, competing against other sports teams).
- Music (e.g., music competitions, trying out for choirs).
- Personal achievements (e.g., only the best artwork or writing examples are displayed).
- Social (e.g., being the most popular).

SLEEP PATTERNS

Children in this age group sleep only at night, for an average of 10 hours per night. They may get up earlier but can amuse themselves without supervision. Bedtime, on the other hand, often becomes a battleground, as children try to extend the time that they are up. Establishing routines, such as encouraging the child to lie in bed and read a book or listen to some music before going to sleep, may help to defuse the situation.

PERSONAL CARE ROUTINES

Younger children in this age group often have a careless attitude toward personal cleanliness and appearance. By the end of this age period, however, they start to become more conscious of their personal appearance and need fewer reminders to tidy up. They may, however, need reminders to wash their hands at appropriate times, clean their fingernails, and wash their necks as well as their faces. Personal care routines need to be continually monitored to help the child develop healthy habits.

Children often have favourite clothing that they want to wear all the time, even if it is dirty. Some children may try to wear a dirty item under clean clothes. Again, careful monitoring is important.

EATING

By the end of this age period, children have developed better eating habits. They have learned appropriate table manners but may still try to hurry through a meal to get back to fun activities. They are becoming more interested in food and are willing to try new foods.

INCREASED ABSTRACT THOUGHT STAGE

Children start to be less dependent on realism to solve problems and manipulate materials in their environments.

Increased Independence
- Independent in self-care routines
- Needs guidelines from adults

Changing Interests
- More focused on long-term activities (e.g., reading a book) or learning a skill (e.g., skating)

Forming of Friendships
- Social interactions
- Maintenance of friendships

Competition
- Understand rules
- Engage in competitive sports or games, such as hockey or Monopoly

Physical Activity
- Increased ability to control fine and gross motor abilities
- Fine and gross motor abilities become increasingly refined

Formal Education
- Attend school
- Increased need to learn through reading, writing, and abstract reasoning, such as computation

Cooperation
- Work with others to plan and reach goals, such as working on a project

Self-Concept
Dependent on:
- How others view self
- Personal abilities

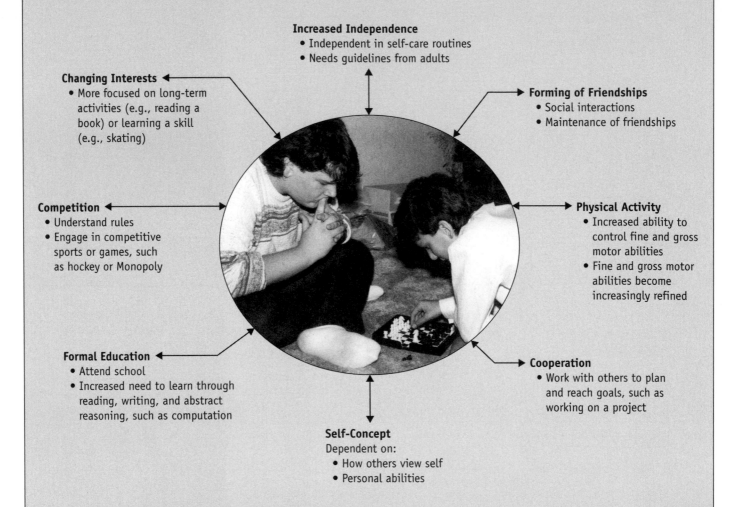

CHAPTER 11

Six Years

"I was so scared on my first day in grade one. Then it was OK because my best friend was in my class. I got to go on a houseboat trip with him. We had a lot of fun."

PHOTO 11.1 At six, children's agility and coordination continue to improve.

INTRODUCTION

Six-year-olds face major changes in their lives. Grade 1 is much more formal than kindergarten, with increased expectations. In fact, many of the new school-based activities are considered by most experts in the world as developmentally inappropriate for six-year-olds (Gestwicki, 1999; Elkind, 1988).

As skills become integrated and consolidated, new challenges appear and are embraced enthusiastically. At times, attempts to meet these challenges end in frustration because children may not be able to perform the tasks or activities at the level they expect. Children of this age also face an increased number of choices in their daily lives that can be both rewarding and, at times, overwhelming.

PHYSICAL DEVELOPMENT

Six-year-olds have learned to control and integrate fine and gross motor skills. They can manipulate painting tools to create small intricate drawings and also use large sweeping motions to fill a page. These activities require the integration of wrist, finger, and arm movements.

Children in this age group usually exhibit increased creativity in using a variety of skills in writing, music and movement, and art activities. Many children have either started or will now start formal lessons in dance, music, or gross motor activities, such as swimming, gymnastics, and skating.

TABLE 11.1	Gross Motor Development—6 Years	
SKILL	**DESCRIPTION**	**☀ DEVELOPMENTAL ALERT**
Movement	• Uses controlled movements to run, jump, twist, bend, turn body, throw, and catch • Continues to improve in speed, strength, agility, and coordination (Photo 11.1) • Has increased interest in and ability at sports, such as swimming, baseball, soccer, and hockey • Can ride a bicycle	Movements remain disjointed, clumsy

TABLE 11.2	Fine Motor Development—6 Years	
SKILL	**DESCRIPTION**	**☀ DEVELOPMENTAL ALERT**
Overall	• Tripod grasp firmly established • Has greater control to write, trace, cut, colour inside lines, form clay or play dough objects • Sometimes works on creative projects over time, both alone and in group situations	Lack of control in drawing, painting, writing

TABLE 11.2	Fine Motor Development—6 Years *(continued)*	
SKILL	**DESCRIPTION**	✳ **DEVELOPMENTAL ALERT**
Artwork	• Combines several art activities to create one product (e.g., tracing, cutting, colouring, and gluing) • Produces recognizable symbolic representations (Photo 11.2) • Provides greater detail in drawings (e.g., rays on the sun, petals and leaves on flowers) • Starts to use colours more deliberately (e.g., colours eyes blue because the person depicted has blue eyes) • Begins to scale the sizes of items more realistically (e.g., flowers are smaller than a house, and trees are larger than flowers) • Human figures become more detailed (e.g., five fingers on hands, hair on the head, features on the face) (Crowther, 2003)	Lack of recognizable symbolic representations

COGNITIVE DEVELOPMENT

Children in this age group are increasingly more able to use abstract thought and representation. They are able to read, write, perform mathematical functions, and express themselves by playing musical instruments or engaging in dance activities.

PHOTO 11.2 Six-year-olds' drawings usually contain recognizable symbolic representations.

TABLE 11.3	Cognitive Development—6 Years	
SKILL	**DESCRIPTION**	**✳ DEVELOPMENTAL ALERT**
Decentration (quantity, mass, length)	• *Quantity:* Realizes that the arrangement of two sets of a number of objects does not affect the number of objects in each set (average age: 5–7) • *Mass:* Realizes that altering the shape of a ball of clay does not alter the amount of clay (average age: 6–8) • *Length:* Realizes that altering the shape of a pipe cleaner does not alter its length (average age: 6–8)	Lack of decentration
Attention span	Increased attention span while working on problems, projects, creative activities; may be inconsistent	Short attention span
Abstract thinking	Has developed the skill to think and understand concepts that are more abstract and complex (e.g., understands about death and dying, pregnancy)	Does not show understanding of abstract concepts
Concept development	• *Size:* Measures to identify which item is longer, which weighs more • *Seriation:* Can arrange 5–10 objects in descending or ascending order • *Numbers:* Knows numbers up to 10, performs addition and subtraction using concrete numbers; forms sets of equal numbers; matches symbols to numbers • *Time:* Understands time in relation to today, tomorrow, yesterday; understands seasons and seasonal changes (fall, winter, spring, summer); identifies hour times, but may still become confused • *Money:* Identifies which amount of money will buy more • *Sorting:* Sorts objects using more than one dimension (e.g., finds all toy animals with hoofs)	• Difficulty understanding concepts • Continues to sort by one dimension only
Counting	• Counts up to 10 objects; may not be consistent • Rote counts to 100 • May rote count by 10 or 2 or 5 to 100, but may skip numbers or substitute incorrect numbers	Inability to count objects
Thinking	Starts to think more independently and develops own opinions as information is received from peers, adults, books, and the media	Thinking based only on concrete situations

LANGUAGE DEVELOPMENT

At this age, children become more proficient at using alternative modes of communication, as reading and writing abilities increase with age. There are great variations in when children start to read and how well they read; this often depends on previous exposure to books. Children who come from homes that encourage reading tend to become more proficient readers.

The Grade 1 standard reading program is imposed on all children, although not all children complete this program in one year. This means that by the time these children are eight years old, they may be significantly below the expected reading and writing levels.

TABLE 11.4 Language Development—6 Years

SKILL	DESCRIPTION	✳ DEVELOPMENTAL ALERT
Conversation	• Talking has become a major event—with peers, with adults; may interrupt, in excitement to talk • Uses language to express dissatisfaction, frustration, anger • Imitates and initiates slang, profanities • Uses humour to attract attention—tells jokes, riddles, and makes up funny stories • Makes up stories to tell peers and adults	Conversations disjointed, do not make sense
Grammar	Appropriate use of: • Verb tenses • Word order • Sentence structure	Inappropriate use of grammar
Vocabulary	• Knows 10 000 to 14 000 words • Learns 5–10 new words per day	
Writing	• Writes more words, simple sentences, simple stories • Uses letters and phonics to reproduce words, such as "RANBO" ("rainbow") • Uses traditional spelling in writing (e.g., the Canadian spelling of words) • May neglect to put space between words, so they run together • Common errors include omission of silent letters or double letters, and substitutions, such as "f" for "ph" • Often reverses letters or words (e.g., was and saw)	Few attempts to write
Reading concepts	• Masters concept of reading from left to right, top to bottom by end of sixth year • Readily discerns differences between most letters and words, but confuses letters and words that are similar; most children do a combination of both • Has difficulty picking up context clues while reading • Understands the meaning of appropriate material read and can answer questions about it • Can identify initial, medial, and final phonic sounds in words • Starts to understand punctuation	• No interest in reading • Struggles to read individual words
Reading style	• Reads one word at a time; more fluency at end of sixth year • Sounds out words to read • Reads words from memory • May use finger to follow reading • Corrects self if a word does not make sense	

PERSONAL/SOCIAL DEVELOPMENT

Peer relationships become very important during these early school years. Children form close friendships and start to interact with larger groups of friends. Friendships may still be transient—a best friend today may be a worst enemy tomorrow.

TABLE 11.5	Personal/Social Development—6 Years	
SKILL	**DESCRIPTION**	✳ **DEVELOPMENTAL ALERT**
Emotional control	• Anxious to please • Seeks approval for activities or tasks completed • May show some egocentric tendencies by perceiving some situations from one perspective only • Starts to understand that people may act differently from how they are feeling • Moods swing from dependent and lovable to independent and uncooperative • Improved self-control, conforms to adult ideas of "proper" behaviour and recognizes appropriateness • Easily upset by losing, or by perceived failure • Understands concepts of normality and abnormality; concerned with being normal • Is curious about individual differences	• Lack of self-control • Resorts to aggression rather than verbalization
Peer interactions	• Friendship circles expand, but best friends may become worst enemies • Spends more time with peers • Turn to peers for information	• Few friends • Does not join peer activities
Moral development	• Behaves in accordance with rules and accepts the guidance of authority figures • Often refers to behaviour in terms of extremes—good or bad	
Understanding social situations	• Believes that everything seen is true (e.g., television commercials) • Has difficulty detecting the possibly dangerous intentions of others (e.g. an offer of candy from an adult is perceived as kindly; in reality, the adult may have other intentions)	
Dependency	Less dependent on adults as friendships expand	Dependent on adults

TOOLS FOR OBSERVING—SIX YEARS

A blank version of the observation chart in this section can be downloaded for your use from Nelson's Resource Centre for Early Childhood Education at www.ece. nelson.com.

SAMPLE 1
Interests

The chart below can be used to track a child's current and emergent interests and skills and can assist in identifying:

- Current skill levels.
- Learning challenges that can be posed, based on current interests.
- Future learning activities that will promote skill development.

Interests—6 Years

Name: James

INTEREST	DESCRIPTION	DATE
Reading	Liked books about adventures	Oct. 1
Math	Measured and weighed items, then created a bar graph to compare the objects; worked on this activity for two weeks	Oct. 2–10

SAMPLE 2
Anecdotal Notes

Figure 11.1 shows a series of notes tracking a child's activities. These notes help to identify:

- Milestones.
- Skill levels.
- Future learning activities that can be planned.
- Additional materials and resources to expand learning.

Simply jot down notes as you watch the child's activities, and then organize the notes in a folder under appropriate headings, such as "Math," "Reading," or "Interests."

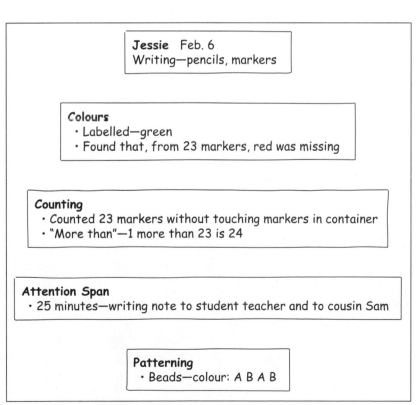

FIGURE 11.1 Anecdotal Notes

Eric, Sept. 23

Match: Number sign to number of objects
Object Count: Able to count out objects to
identify how many

Match	Count
0	
1 |	|
2 |	|
3 |	|
4 |	
5 |	
6 |	|
7 |	
8 |	|
9 |	
10	

Comments:
• Used blocks as rocks.
• Built structure to match number of blocks to
  number on turtle's back.

FIGURE 11.2 Skill Identification

SAMPLE 3
Skill Development

Figure 11.2 shows a simple way to track a child's ability to identify written numerals and to count objects. Counting objects involves the ability to count how many objects are in a set and then state the total number. This chart will help to identify:
• Milestones in any domain, such as reading, phonics, or writing.
• Skill levels.
• Future activities and materials that will expand learning.

REFERENCES

Crowther, I. (2003). *Creating effective learning environments*. Scarborough, ON: Nelson Thomson Learning.

Elkind, D. (1988). *The hurried child*. Don Mills, ON: Addison-Wesley Publishing Company.

Gestwicki, C. (1999). *Developmentally appropriate practices* (2nd ed.). Scarborough, ON: Nelson Canada.

CHAPTER 12

Seven to Eight Years

Children become increasingly more independent between the years of seven and eight and are adjusting to their home and school routines. Peer acceptance and friendships are closely tied to self-esteem and self-worth.

INTRODUCTION

Seven-year-olds have gained greater skill in their ability to stay on task. They have longer attention spans and are more likely to listen to others. Seven-year-olds are also more able and willing to share and cooperate with others. Increased expectations of themselves, at home and at school, may cause them to withdraw from certain situations or strive to do things more perfectly to live up to these expectations. This may lead to frustration and cause stress. Children start to worry about new situations and their ability to do well.

Eight-year-olds have adjusted to school life. Children of this age strive for peer acceptance, and so they are more conscious of their appearance and spend more time getting dressed. They start to emulate fads in clothes and hairstyles. Their language and social interactions are based on what is deemed acceptable by the peer group.

PHYSICAL DEVELOPMENT

Physical development continues to be refined. Children demonstrate their skills through increased ability in printing, can do cursive writing and more detailed artwork, and have greater agility and improved gross motor skill abilities. They participate in organized sports or leisure activities such as tennis, hockey, baseball, ballet, or music.

TABLE 12.1	Gross Motor Development—7–8 Years	
SKILL	**DESCRIPTION**	**✳ DEVELOPMENTAL ALERT**
Movement	• Demonstrates better balance and greater strength, endurance, speed, agility, and coordination in competitive and noncompetitive events • Becomes skilled at a variety of gross motor activities (e.g., skating, skiing, swimming, skateboarding, in-line skating, bike riding, dancing, skipping) • Practises skills to master them (Photo 12.1)	• Movements look awkward/ uncoordinated • Limited participation in physical activities
Sports	• Increased activity in team sports (e.g., baseball, soccer, hockey) • Increased participation in competitive activities (e.g., gymnastics, figure skating)	Limited interest or participation in sports

TABLE 12.2	Fine Motor Development—7–8 Years	
SKILL	**DESCRIPTION**	**✳ DEVELOPMENTAL ALERT**
Writing/game playing	• Writing and drawing marks become smaller • Writing becomes more evenly spaced and more legible • May learn to use cursive writing • Plays games requiring greater dexterity (e.g., jacks, marbles)	Poor coordination; letters appear large and spacing is erratic

TABLE 12.2	**Fine Motor Development—7–8 Years** *(continued)*	
SKILL	**DESCRIPTION**	❋ **DEVELOPMENTAL ALERT**
Artwork	*Schematic achievement of a concept (Crowther, 2003)* • Develops distinct forms and repeats them • Produces flat representations of objects • Produces two-dimensional representations of space • Begins to include base lines and sky (Photo 12.2) • Drawings and paintings reflect child's knowledge of the world • May show exterior or interior details • Draws refined, recognizable human figures • Overall "stiffness" to drawings (Crowther, 2003) • Uses colour deliberately • Forms integrated three-dimensional structures with a variety of materials (e.g., boxes, paper, clay, dough)	Art work continues to reflect earlier symbolized forms

PHOTO 12.1 Children in this age group practise skills to master them.

PHOTO 12.2 Base lines and sky appear in the art of seven- and eight-year-olds.

COGNITIVE DEVELOPMENT

Success in reading is often related to the support and encouragement provided by family members and to the family's socioeconomic status. Unfortunately, many children are significantly behind in reading skills at the end of Grade 3—37 percent of children were not reading at grade level in one large, urban, low-income school district (Reutzel & Cooter, 2000).

TABLE 12.3	Cognitive Development—7–8 Years	
SKILL	**DESCRIPTION**	**✳ DEVELOPMENTAL ALERT**
Decentration	• Decentration in relation to mass, quantity, and length firmly established • Understands that changes in how a surface is covered does not change the basic surface area • Understands that changes in the arrangement of items does not change the original number of items involved	Limited decentration
Abstract thinking	• Begins to understand that others may have different opinions • Begins to understand that people of different cultures may think and live differently (Photo 12.3)	Continues to use egocentric thought processes
Concept development	• *Perspective:* Demonstrates an understanding of perspective in artwork (e.g., shadows, distance, shapes) • *Numbers:* Adds and subtracts multi-digit numbers; starts to perform simple multiplication and division • *Classification:* Sorts and re-sorts into subcategories	Limited understanding of these concepts
Memory	Begins to use rehearsal strategies to remember things (e.g., learning math by adding or subtracting concrete counters, or retracing steps to try to find a misplaced object)	• Forgetful with items • Finds it hard to remember new skills

PHOTO 12.3 Seven- and eight-year-olds begin to understand that people of different cultures may think and live differently.

LANGUAGE DEVELOPMENT

Language capabilities continue to expand during this period and include a greater ability to initiate and maintain conversations. Children continue to develop their reading and writing skills for a variety of purposes, such as research activities, enjoyment, and exploring different types of literature.

TABLE 12.4	Language Development—7–8 Years	
SKILL	**DESCRIPTION**	**✳ DEVELOPMENTAL ALERT**
Conversation	• Continues to enjoy jokes and riddles • Uses and enjoys word plays, such as puns • Speaks fluently • Talks to friends on the telephone • Imitates colloquial language (e.g., slang words, swear words, curses) • Compliments and criticizes others	• Limited conversation with peers or others • Conversations hard to follow
Grammar	Understands and follows grammatical rules in conversation and in writing	Poor grammar
Vocabulary	• Enjoys learning new words, especially longer ones • Looks up words in a dictionary	Limited repertoire of words
Writing	• Uses writing in everyday tasks at school • Writes letters or notes to friends • Leaves notes or takes messages in writing • Uses conventional spelling	• Limited interest in writing • Many words misspelled
Reading	• Reads for a purpose (e.g., to find information, for enjoyment) • Becomes a more fluent reader	• Reading is hesitant and slow • Does not understand what has been read

PERSONAL/SOCIAL DEVELOPMENT

Seven- and eight-year-olds have a much greater awareness of themselves as individuals. They continually strive toward self-improvement but may have unrealistic expectations. Children try very hard to meet expectations, which could lead to stress in relation to an upcoming assignment, test, or event.

TABLE 12.5　Personal/Social Development—7–8 Years

SKILL	DESCRIPTION	✳ DEVELOPMENTAL ALERT
Emotional control	• Less critical of self • Easily frustrated if unable to complete tasks that meet expectations • Verbalizes praise and criticism of self and others • Recognizes abilities and shortcomings of others (e.g., enhanced ability in art or music, lack of ability in spelling or reading) • Requires attention and acknowledgement of efforts from adults, but may not ask for it • Understands more complex emotions (e.g., confusion and excitement) • Has increased ability to control and conceal feelings • Requires more emotional freedom and space from parents	• Critical of self • Poor self-concept
Peer interactions	• Joins team or group activities (Photo 12.4) • Has two or three best friends • Engages in some solitary activities (e.g., reading, walking) • Understands that others may interpret information differently, but thinks it is due to different information • Develops relationships with people outside the family	• Engages in solitary activities • Has difficulty forming and maintaining friendships
Moral development	• Lives up to expectations of close individuals • Identifies with "being good" • Understands the difference between good and bad • Shows concern for others	Does not understand the difference between good and bad
Personal characteristics	• Becomes increasingly modest • Requires more privacy • Expresses love and affection through talking and sharing; may be embarrassed by physical affection	
Sexual development	• Socializes more with same gender • Respects taboos surrounding sexuality • Understands more about sexuality and that there are different reasons for intercourse • Gathers information about sex from outside sources (e.g., peers, media, books) • Understands gender role stereotypes • Has developed a stronger self-concept of gender	

PHOTO 12.4 Group and team activities are usually enjoyed by children in this age group.

TOOLS FOR OBSERVING—SEVEN–EIGHT YEARS

Blank versions of the observation charts in this section can be downloaded for your use from Nelson's Resource Centre for Early Childhood Education at www.ece.nelson.com.

SAMPLE 1
Skill Set

The chart below can be used to record observations of skills in any area—physical, social, emotional, and social—and will help to identify:

- Milestones.
- Level of skills.
- Beneficial future learning activities.
- Resources that could be provided to improve or enhance skills.

Educators can use these charts to prepare reports for families or for teachers in the children's next grade. Always give each chart a title, and then use that chart only for the type of observation identified in that title. This provides continuity while observing the child's progress and makes it easier to interpret what you have observed.

Cognitive Development: Decentration—7–8 Years

Name:

SKILL	DESCRIPTION	DATE
Mass (conservation of mass)	Divided dough into two balls and stated, "I now have two balls. This one and that one (pointing to the two dough balls) are the same as the one I started with."	Oct. 1

SAMPLE 2
Reading Record

This chart helps to identify:

- How much reading has been done.
- Current interests.
- Other books that could be provided to encourage reading.

Reading Record—7–8 Years

Name:

BOOK READ	READING LEVEL	COMMENTS	DATE

REFERENCES

Crowther, I. (2003). *Creating effective learning environments*. Scarborough, ON: Nelson Thomson Learning.

Reutzel, D., & Cooter, R. (2000). *Teaching children to read*. Upper Saddle River, NJ: Pearson Education.

THE PRETEEN YEARS

Nine to Twelve

INTRODUCTION

The preteen years from 9 to 12 are marked by a number of milestones, including:

- Formation of enduring friendships.
- Greater ability to use abstract thought.
- Greater independence and use of initiative.
- Refinement of all motor control leading to greater ability to participate in a variety of activities (e.g., sports, music, art).
- Refined academic skills (e.g., reading, writing) resulting in more independent thinking.
- Development of hobbies and interests related to the development and refinement of all skills and abilities (e.g., playing chess, developing and organizing collections, such as hockey cards or stamps, reading for pleasure).

GROWTH PATTERNS

Children in this age group usually gain about 90 percent on average of the weight they will acquire before they stop growing. Growth spurts for girls occur between the ages of 10 and 11; for boys, this usually happens between 13 and 14. Weight gain during this period is related more to muscle gain than to fat and leads to tremendous growth in strength. Boys develop more muscle cells than do girls and are therefore stronger than girls during this period.

Unfortunately, many children become inactive and develop poor eating habits during this critical growth period. Sedentary family lifestyles and long hours of sitting at a school desk, watching TV, or playing video games at home, combined with poor eating habits, may lead to obesity, especially in girls.

This time period is usually marked by the onset of puberty, and children experience body changes, such as the growth of pubic hair in both genders, and breast development and the onset of menstruation in girls. Menstruation begins on average between the ages of 11 and 12; some girls start earlier and others start later, which has been known to cause depression in girls who think an earlier or later start is not "normal."

BRAIN DEVELOPMENT

As refined abstract thinking emerges, another brain spurt can be detected. During this period, additional milestones in brain development occur:

- **Lateralization**—certain functions, such as speech, language, or creativity, become located in a specific hemisphere of the brain
- Increased myelination, which speeds up the rate of transmission of neural impulses
- Continued pruning of neural connections, which increases the brain's efficiency

lateralization
development of dominance in one or both cerebral hemispheres with regard to specific functions, such as speech, language, or creativity

COGNITIVE GROWTH

An increased ability to think in more abstract ways provides children in this age group with a greater capacity to solve problems by themselves (e.g., to use reading and writing skills in researching problems and documenting solutions). Greater knowledge of science and math concepts provides opportunities to solve problems in a number of ways, trying different methods if one way does not work.

COMMUNICATION

Children in this age group usually read and communicate well, and use writing to express themselves. Symbolized creative forms are used for music, dance, science, and math (e.g., musical notes, body movements, mathematical and scientific symbols).

PERSONAL/SOCIAL DEVELOPMENT

Preteens spend a lot of time with friends, often in small groups. These groups interact on a regular basis, share similar values and interests, and support each other emotionally. Cliques may be formed.

CHAPTER 13

Nine to Twelve Years

During the preteen years, children develop more independence. Preteens usually become very conscious of their appearance and will try to blend in with their particular peer group. They often use peer-recognized language and mannerisms, and adapt their personal appearance (hair styles, clothes, possibly body piercing) to fit in with those of their friends. This may cause the preteen to be in conflict with family members or other individuals in authority.

INTRODUCTION

The preteen years are a social time. Children begin to form more lasting friendships and friendships with peers of the opposite gender. Peer groups become more important, and as a result, children become more independent with regard to family relationships but may switch back to dependency at times.

PHYSICAL DEVELOPMENT

Preteens have developed a wide range of abilities and skills, but these years are also marked by greater variations among children in the area of physical abilities and fitness. Children involved in active sport programs or other recreational activities may be full of energy and physically fit, but many Canadian preteens are overweight and lack overall fitness.

TABLE 13.1	Gross Motor Development—9–12 Years	
SKILL	**DESCRIPTION**	✳ **DEVELOPMENTAL ALERT**
Reaction	• Reacts more quickly, which increases ability to participate in sports • Adept at ball skills (e.g., dribbling, running, aiming kick)	• Clumsy or uncoordinated • Lack of interest in physical activity
Pride in accomplishments	Shows confidence and pride in gross motor skills (Photo 13.1)	

TABLE 13.2	Fine Motor Development—9–12 Years	
SKILL	**DESCRIPTION**	✳ **DEVELOPMENTAL ALERT**
Dexterity	Demonstrates improved fine motor dexterity in activities such as model-building, art, sculpting, sewing, weaving	Has difficulty with activities involving dexterity
Writing	Cursive writing or printing used as needed	Writing difficult to read
Creativity	• Provides more detail in all types of creative activities (e.g., painting, sculpting, dioramas) (Photo 13.2) • Understands the required scale of items in art, can portray distance • Experiments with an increased variety of media (e.g., ink sketches, bas relief, etchings)	Limited interest in creative activities

COGNITIVE DEVELOPMENT

Growth in cognitive abilities during the preteen years is demonstrated by the ability to read increasingly more complex information; write coherent passages; engage in abstract activities, such as mental computation; create complex plots for dramatic plays; and demonstrate a greater understanding of the world around them.

PHOTO 13.1 Preteens usually have confidence in their physical skills and are proud of their accomplishments.

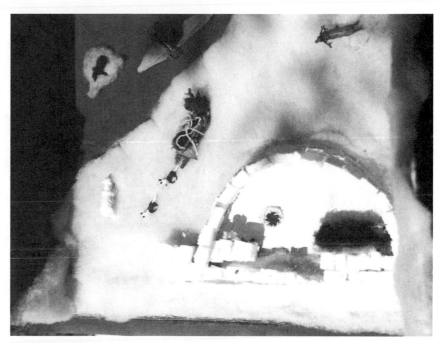

PHOTO 13.2 Preteens' art shows higher levels of detail.

TABLE 13.3	**Cognitive Development—9–12 Years**	
SKILL	**DESCRIPTION**	☀ **DEVELOPMENTAL ALERT**
Decentration	*Volume:* Starts to understand that different shapes of containers can hold the same amount of liquid	
Abstract thought	• Recognizes which details are important and which ones can be eliminated when talking or when working on projects • Less reliant on concrete experiences to formulate solutions to problems or ideas • Increased skill in summarizing and creating outlines to plan projects or assignments	• Includes all details • Thinking is limited by a situation or concrete materials

LANGUAGE DEVELOPMENT

Many preteens are competent communicators. They have developed skills to initiate and maintain conversations and are able to argue points effectively. They may start to reference their discussions (verbal and written) to books or articles they have read, favourite movies or television programs, or personal heroes they have heard about or observed.

Abilities in the communication area vary greatly among preteens; for example, reading skills may range from illiteracy to near-adult competency.

TABLE 13.4	Language Skills—9–12 Years	
SKILL	**DESCRIPTION**	**❋ DEVELOPMENTAL ALERT**
Reading	Reads fluently	• Poor reading or comprehension skills • Avoidance of reading activities
Writing	• Some write fluently, creatively; others are not very skilled at writing • Experiments with various styles of writing (e.g., prose, poetry, fiction, adventure stories)	• Poor spelling • Difficult to understand writing

PERSONAL/SOCIAL DEVELOPMENT

Preteens are very aware of themselves in a social context. They try to blend in with their chosen group of friends. Attraction to the opposite sex begins to emerge.

TABLE 13.5	Personal/Social Development—9–12 Years	
SKILL	**DESCRIPTION**	**❋ DEVELOPMENTAL ALERT**
Emotional control	• Aware of own feelings and the feelings of others • May start to feel attracted to the opposite sex	• Poor emotional control
Viewpoints	• Has independent viewpoints • Defends viewpoints with arguments based on experience and knowledge • Has difficulty detecting deceptions of others (untruths, advertising gimmicks)	Easily swayed by peers
Moral development	Begins to understand that all things may not be good or bad, that there are degrees of each	Continues to think of things as good or bad only
Independence	• Requires more independence from family • Challenges rules and expectations	Dependent on adults and peers
Sexual development	• Expected body changes that occur early or late may cause increased stress • Is more interested in sexual development and asks questions • Has greater awareness of opposite sex	

TOOLS FOR OBSERVING—NINE–TWELVE YEARS

The observation charts presented in the other chapters, particularly in the last three chapters, are equally appropriate for use for this age group. Blank versions of all of the observation charts that appeared previously can be downloaded for your use from Nelson's Resource Centre for Early Childhood Education at www.ece.nelson.com.

APPENDIX A

Developmental Milestones

This appendix presents developmental milestones in curricular areas, such as block play and sand play, and developmental areas, such as grasping. Photographs of key developmental milestones for grasp and object permanence are provided, as well as ages-and-stages charts and illustrations of a range of activities, from sand play to woodworking. (Please note: Photos appear in the order of emergence of development.)

DEVELOPMENTAL AREAS

Photo Gallery: Grasp

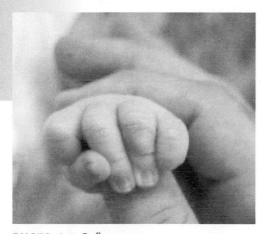

PHOTO A.1 Reflex grasp

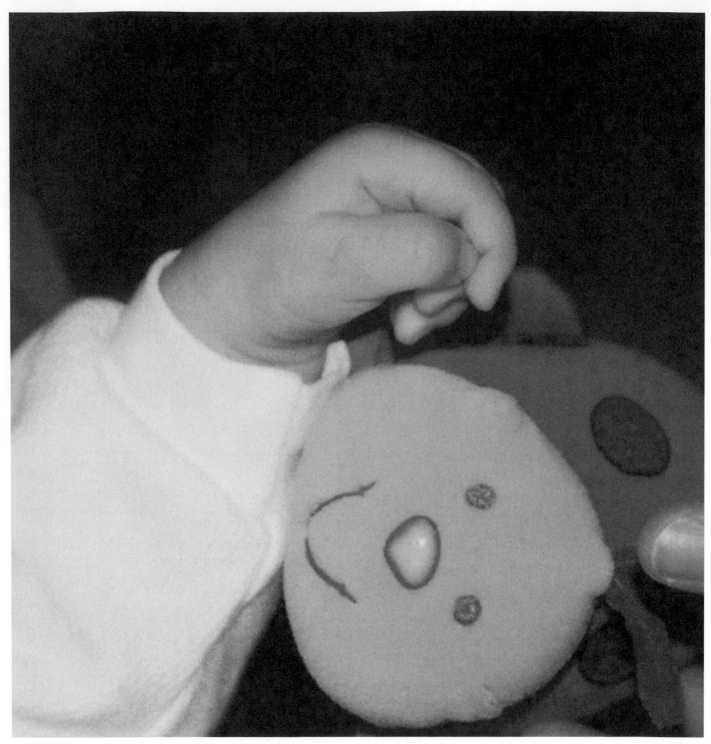

PHOTO A.2 Primitive holding grasp

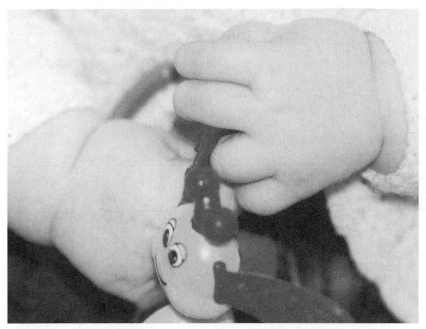

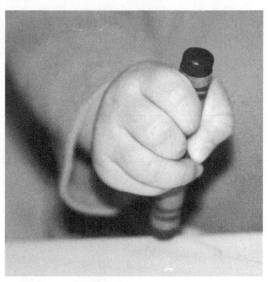

PHOTO A.3 Transfer from hand to hand

PHOTO A.4 Palmar grasp

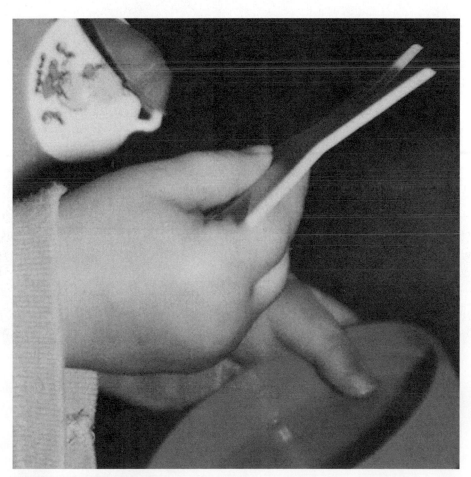

PHOTO A.5 Pincer grasp

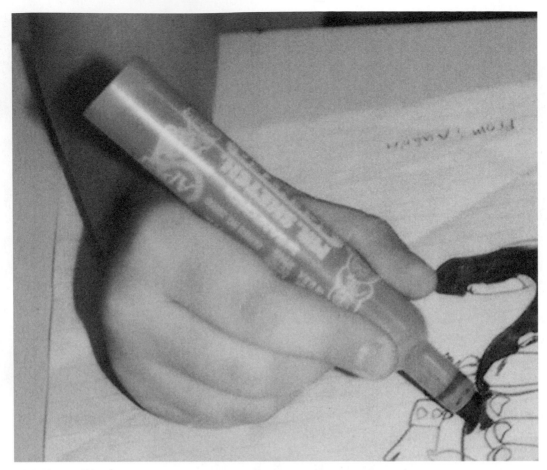

PHOTO A.6 Tripod grasp

Photo Gallery: Object Permanence

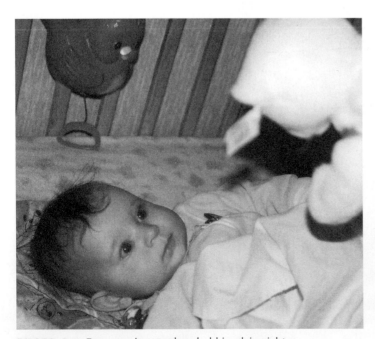

PHOTO A.7 Focus on items when held in plain sight

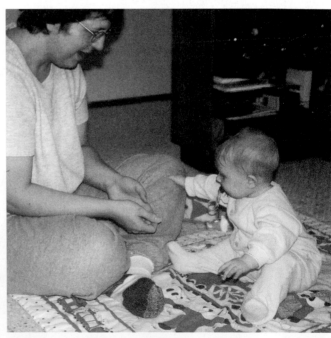

PHOTO A.8 Look for object where last seen

PHOTO A.9 Look for objects when hidden

PHOTO A.10 Look for hidden objects in new places

CURRICULAR AREAS

TABLE A.1	Comparison of Ages and Stages of Social and Cognitive Play
Infants	
Solitary Play	Play by themselves
	Initially play involves using hands, feet, and mouth
	As infants mature, they grasp and manipulate toys (Photo A.11, p. 199)
Onlooker Behaviour	Watch other individuals in their environment
	Focus on objects near them
Parallel Play	Older, more mobile infants will play close to each other, using similar materials and engaging in similar activities
Functional Play	Play involves much repetition
	Infants engage in manipulation of objects—poking, prodding, pushing, pulling, turning, and twisting (Photo A.17, p. 202)
	Older infants will start to use realistic objects as intended—cups to drink, spoons to feed

Table A.1 continues on next page

TABLE A.1 Comparison of Ages and Stages of Social and Cognitive Play

Toddlers

Onlooker Behaviour	Attention easily attracted by activity of other toddlers Toddlers will leave own activity to see what is happening elsewhere
Solitary Play	If interested in the activity, will continue to play by self for long periods of time
Parallel Play	Often play beside other individuals, without interactions, using similar toys and engaging in similar activities (Photo A.12)
Functional Play	Engage in repetitive play, especially if the play experience is a new one Engage in activities that focus on emptying, filling, taking apart, stacking, and knocking down (Photo A.18, p. 202)
Symbolic Play	Start to use one object to represent another object Play is rich in symbolic actions (Photo A.19, p. 203)

Preschoolers

Onlooker Behaviour	May watch new experiences to see if they wish to participate May watch play, if unsure of self or situation
Solitary Play	Will play by self by choice to explore new situations or simply to be alone for a while
Parallel Play	May play side by side if child becomes absorbed in what he or she is doing
Associative Play	Often play along with others, sharing toys and ideas but continuing to do own thing (Photo A.13, p. 200)
Functional Play	May resort to functional play to explore unknown situations or activities
Constructive Play	Readily use available materials to substitute materials not available Engage in many symbolic actions—raising hand for stop, shrugging shoulders to indicate uncertainty (Photo A.23, p. 204)
Dramatic Play	Often become involved in role-play and/or imaginative play without props (Photos A.20, p. 203; A.25, p. 205)

School Age

Will engage in all types of play depending on interest, mood, inclination, setting, and materials (Photos A.16, p. 201; A.21, p. 203; A.24, p. 205)	
Cooperative Play	Start to play with peers to organize play activities Activities include working toward a common goal, planning and assigning roles to reach the goal (Photo A.14, p. 200)
Competitive Play	Children become increasingly competitive (Photo A.15, p. 201) Play includes winning and losing
Games with Rules	Children may set own rules for their play Engage in activities that have increasingly complex sets of rules—team sports, board games

Photo Gallery: Social Play

PHOTO A.11 Infants and toddlers—solitary play

PHOTO A.12 Toddlers and preschoolers—parallel play

PHOTO A.13 Toddlers and preschoolers—associative play

PHOTO A.14 Preschoolers and school age—cooperative play

PHOTO A.15 School age—competitive games

PHOTO A.16 Early infancy and throughout stages—onlooker behaviour

Photo Gallery: Cognitive Play

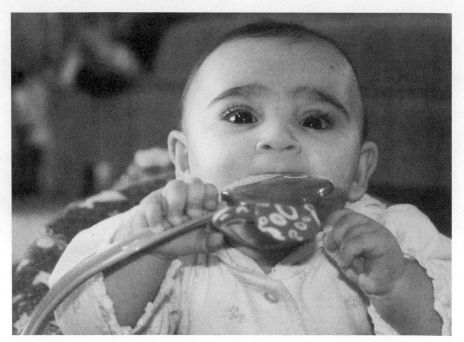

PHOTO A.17 Infants—functional play

PHOTO A.18 Toddlers—functional play

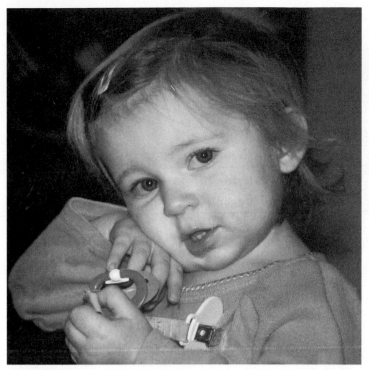

PHOTO A.19 Late infancy—symbolic play

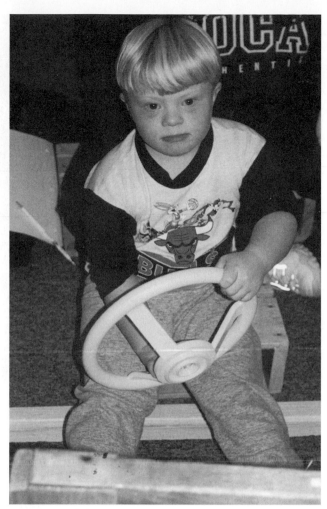

PHOTO A.20 Preschoolers—symbolic play

PHOTO A.21 School age—symbolic play

PHOTO A.22 Toddlers—constructive play

PHOTO A.23 Preschoolers—constructive play

PHOTO A.24 School age—constructive play

PHOTO A.25 Late toddlers, preschoolers, school age—dramatic play

TABLE A.2   Comparison of Ages and Stages of Water Play

PHASE	AGE	BEHAVIOURS
Free exploration	Infants	Bath time—splashing with hands and feet when held
		Bath time, sensory water pools—sit in water, grab water toys within reach, put in mouth
		Water pools, hose, sprinklers—drop things in water, put things into floating toys, take them out repeatedly; crawl, run through water sprinklers, climb into pool
		Solitary or parallel play
		Sensory, functional play (Photo A.26)
Free exploration	Toddlers	Walk, run through puddles, run through sprinklers, jump into water, splash repeatedly
		Water table—drop things; float items; pour water into containers, dump water out repeatedly
		Blow bubbles, chase bubbles, repeatedly
		Bathe "babies," self-care routines—wash hands, brush teeth
		Wash dishes
		Solitary or parallel play, functional play with toys
		Symbolized actions (Photo A.27)
Experiment to make connections	Preschool, ages 3–5	Solitary, parallel, associative play
		Talk about what is happening, share discoveries with adults, peers, delight in new discoveries
		Drop things into the water, into containers in the water
		Pour, squirt, empty, fill repeatedly
		Wash dolls, clothing, tables, clean floor with mop, clean easels
		Spray sand, create water pictures with spray outside
		Create mixtures—mud pies, play dough
		Cook—soups, cakes, cookies (real and pretend)
		Role-play—firefighter, cook, family member roles
		Explore outside during rain, fog, snow—curious about various weather conditions (Photo A.28, p. 208)
Extend knowledge to solve problems	Older preschool and school age	Measure amount of rainfall
		Create, rivers, ponds, lakes
		Create changes of state—freeze, melt, create steam
		Create methods to transport a variety of materials of various weights
		Create various methods to make water flow
		Work to create various types of solutions (saturated, supersaturated) to create new products (crystals) (Photo A.29, p. 208)

PHOTO A.26 Infants—free exploration

PHOTO A.27 Toddlers—free exploration

PHOTO A.28 Older toddlers and preschoolers—experiment to make connections

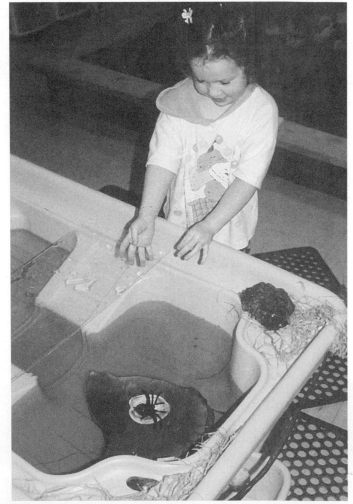

PHOTO A.29 Older preschoolers and school age—Extend knowledge and solve problems

TABLE A.3 Ages and Stages of Music

STAGE	AGE	POSSIBLE BEHAVIOURS
Prenatal		Detectable movement—kicking, poking, relaxing
Listening stage	Infants	Comforted by music Preference for melodic sounds Like soothing music to fall asleep to Listen to songs about everyday routines—diapering, feeding, bathing Find steady rhythms soothing, such as heartbeat, clock Turn eyes or head toward sound Turn body toward sound, wave hands, feet
Imitative	Infants/ toddlers	Initiate or imitate body movements to respond to music Initiate or imitate voice responses—hum, croon, single words, phrases, simple songs Respond to rhythmic movement initiated by self or adult—bounces, claps Imitate rhythms Have favourite songs, ask for many repetitions Can discriminate among different songs Enjoy making sounds with musical instruments or other objects in the environment
Experimental	Toddlers/ preschoolers	Enjoy experimenting with sound—instruments and sound-making objects Regular beat established Sing familiar tunes—alone or in groups, not always in same pitch Create own words to songs or own melodies Use whole body to music—jump, run, tiptoe, walk Dramatize songs
Discovery	Preschool, school age	Reproduce sounds, tones, rhythmic patterns Greater vocal range Create new words to known songs Demonstrate understanding of tempo, volume, and pitch in singing and playing instruments Prefer active participation Enjoy silly or nonsense songs Reproduce melody Play instruments accurately Write and read music Enjoy greater variety of songs—group songs, response songs, silly songs Definite musical preference Coordinate two movements at same time—marching and keeping beat on instrument

Table A.3 continues on next page

TABLE A.3 — Ages and Stages of Music

STAGE	AGE	POSSIBLE BEHAVIOURS
Application	School age	Read music and lyrics Enjoy simple dances Harmonize—rounds, canons, simple two-part harmony Play an instrument Desire to study dance or a musical instrument Compare more than two sounds

TABLE A.4 — Ages and Stages of Block Play

AGE	SKILLS	TYPES OF BLOCKS
Infants—8 to 12 months	Manipulate blocks (Photo A.30) Transfer block from hand to hand Stack, pile blocks Drop, throw blocks	Soft foam blocks covered with material Small wooden blocks suitable for small hands Hard foam blocks Care must be taken to ensure that blocks are sturdy and will not shred or break if mouthed or thrown
12 to 24 months	Transport, carry blocks from one location to another (Photo A.32) Stack two to four objects Push or pull objects	Soft foam blocks covered with material Small wooden blocks suitable for small hands Hard foam blocks Cardboard boxes Wagons, baskets, carts
2 years old	Carry, transport blocks (Photo A.31) Simple rows and towers	Unit blocks, hollow blocks Blocks from previous ages
3 years old	Easily distracted Enclosures, bridges, may start to name structures (Photo A.33, p. 212) Limit choices (Photo A.34, p. 212)	Provide greater variety of blocks All types
4 years old	Combinations—towers, rows, enclosures, bridges (Photo A.35, p. 212) Use blocks with accessories to engage in dramatic play Use patterns to build Sharing ideas with others Building with others	Large number and variety of blocks to offer opportunities to build in small groups Related books and pictures Large areas to extend play
5 years old	Plan building alone or with others Build realistic structures Add detail to structures—ramps, doors, etc. Use other materials to create signs, roadways Extend building over several days by adapting, adding to structures Engage in dramatic play (Photo A.36, p. 213)	Large variety of blocks Crayons, markers, paper, scissors, play dough to create signs and other accessories Related books and pictures Dedicated space to leave blocks out to extend play over several days

Photo Gallery: Block Play

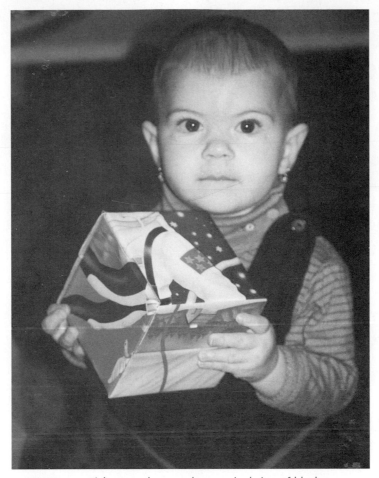

PHOTO A.30 Eight to twelve months—manipulation of blocks

PHOTO A.31 Twelve months to toddlers—transport and carry, simple towers

PHOTO A.32 Two-year-olds— simple rows and towers

PHOTO A.33 Preschoolers to three-year-olds—enclosures

PHOTO A.34 Preschoolers to three-year-olds—bridging

PHOTO A.35 Preschoolers to four-year-olds—combinations

PHOTO A.36 Five-year-olds and up—age representation

TABLE A.5	Ages, Stages, and Books		
LISTING INCLUDES DIVERSITY IN RACE, GENDER, AND CULTURE			
AGE	**SKILL**	**BEHAVIOUR**	**EXAMPLES**
Infants up to 6 months	Listen and look	Facial expression, body movement—arms and legs to show excitement, eye contact with book	Simple picture books that have bright contrast, have single image, and are familiar to the child—easy to create yourself Simple nursery rhymes—especially to do with body parts
Infants 6–12 months	Listen, look by self, identify pictures	Turn pages, get own book, indicate preference through body language, babbling, and first words Point to pictures to identify (Photo A.37, p. 217)	Board books, simple bright pictures, familiar topics, simple stories, simple nursery rhymes Dyer, J. (1986). *Moo, Moo, Peekaboo!* New York, NY: Random House. Argueta, B., & Lousada, S. (1998). *Baby Faces.* New York, NY: Dutton Children's Books.

Table A.5 continues on next page

TABLE A.5   Ages, Stages, and Books

LISTING INCLUDES DIVERSITY IN RACE, GENDER, AND CULTURE

AGE	SKILL	BEHAVIOUR	EXAMPLES
Infants 12–18 months	Identify pictures Recognize books/stories	Identify through pointing Increased ability to verbally identify Repeated requests for same story Chooses and brings book to be read	Board books, picture books; simple story lines; expanded content; simple language; lots of repetition; simple nursery rhymes Argueta, B. & Lousada, S. (1998). *Playing with Pets.* New York, NY: Dutton Children's Books. Butler, J. (2001). *Whose Baby Am I?* New York, NY: Penguin Putman Books for Young Readers. Yoon, S. (1999). *Foil Fun Colors.* Santa Monica, CA: Piggy Toes Press.
Toddlers	Follow story (Photo A.38, p. 218) Read by self Established preference	Independent choice Repetitive—same story over and over again; enjoys stories about things evolving around him/her—new baby in the family, daddy's/mommy's work Intensely curious about things, animals, vehicles	Picture books with detail; simple stories with lots of action; repetitive; rhyming elements Volkmann, R. (2001). *Curious Kitten.* New York, NY: Random House Children's Books. Martin & Carle. (1991). *Polar Bear, Polar Bear, What Do You Hear?* New York, NY: Henry Holdt and Company, LLC. Kopper, L. (1994). *I'm a Baby, You're a Baby.* London, UK: Penguin Books Ltd.
Preschool and school age	Research—look up information Level of search more sophisticated with age Increase vocabulary	Look for pictures Look for words to spell Look for identifying features—shape, colour, size Look for ideas Use dictionaries; ask meanings of words; learn meaning of words from picture clues and from context of story (Photo A.39, p. 218; A.41, p. 219)	Realistic pictures to help identify words; dictionaries Valat, Perols, Jeunesse, & Bourgoing. (1989). *Colours.* London, UK: Moonlight Publishing Ltd. Watts, B. (1991). *See How They Grow: Duck.* Richmond Hill, ON: Scholastic Ltd. Evans, D., & Williams, C. (1992). *How Things Work.* New York, NY: Dorling Kindersley Ltd. Ardley, N. (1995). *How Things Work.* New York, NY: Dorling Kindersley Ltd. Browne, P. (1996). *A Gaggle of Geese.* New York, NY: Simon and Schuster Books for Young Readers.

TABLE A.5 Ages, Stages, and Books

LISTING INCLUDES DIVERSITY IN RACE, GENDER, AND CULTURE

AGE	SKILL	BEHAVIOUR	EXAMPLES
Preschool and school age	Sing a book	Follow words in book as listening to song	Adams, P. (1973). *There Was an Old Lady Who Swallowed a Fly.* Singapore: Child's Play International. Rodgers, R., Hammerstein, O., & Warhola, J. (1994). *My Favorite Things.* New York, NY: Simon and Schuster Books for Young Readers.
Preschool and school age	Look for detail	Look for items hidden in a busy background	Picture books with a lot of detail; find hidden object books Fowler, R. (1995). *There It Is.* London, UK: Campbell Books.
Beginning readers	Read easy-reading books Repetitive, pre-dictable text Predict sequence	Read some words, memorize story and read, sound out words, put in words through context, look at pictures to recognize words (Photo A.40, p. 219)	Repetitive books with pictures to illustrate story; simple words Druce, A., & Ludlow, P. (1998). *Witch, Witch Come to My Party.* Auburn, ME: Child's Play International. Cater, D. *In a Dark, Dark Wood.* New York, NY: Simon and Schuster Books for Young Readers. Brown, R. (1988). *A Dark, Dark Tale.* Toronto, ON: Stoddart Publishing Co. Ltd. Charlip, R. (1964). *Fortunately.* New York, NY: Macmillan Pub. Co. Cheyette Lewison, W., & Wijngaard, J. (1999). *Going to Sleep on the Farm.* New York, NY: Dial Books for Young Readers.
Preschool and school age	Identify feelings	Label feelings from picture Empathize with char-acter, event Relate feelings to own feelings Read and discuss feelings	Short stories with related pictures; stories with moral dilemmas Dijs, C. (1996). *Daddy Would You Love Me If . . .?* New York, NY: Simon and Schuster Books for Young Readers. Joosse, B., & Lavallee, B. (1991). *Mama, Do You Love Me?* Vancouver, BC: Raincoast Books. Harris, P. *Looking at Opposites: Hot Cold, Shy Bold.* Toronto, ON: Kids Can Press Ltd. Gilmore, R., & Sauve, G. (1999). *A Screaming Kind of Day.* Markham, ON: Fitzhenry & Whiteside Ltd.

Table A.5 continues on next page

TABLE A.5 Ages, Stages, and Books

LISTING INCLUDES DIVERSITY IN RACE, GENDER, AND CULTURE

AGE	SKILL	BEHAVIOUR	EXAMPLES
Preschool and school age	Learn alphabet Counting; comparisons	Count objects Recite alphabet Identify colours, objects, shapes	Selsam, M. & Donnelly M. (1995). *Big Tracks, Little Tracks: Following Animal Prints.* New York, NY: HarperCollins. Brown, R. (2001). *Ten Seeds.* London, UK: Anderson Press Ltd. Jeunesse, G. and de Bourgoing, P. *Colours.* London, UK: Moonlight Publishing Ltd. Base, G. (2001). *The Water Hole.* Toronto, ON: Doubleday Canada. Johnson, S. (1995). *Alphabet City.* Toronto, ON: Penguin Books Canada Ltd.
Preschool and early school age	Recognize opposites, differences—appreciate classic stories from different viewpoints	Recognize opposites—first gross differences, leading to minute differences in the school-age years	Picture books with clear opposites Thompson, M., & Newland, G. (1999). *Make a Change Opposites.* Brookfield, CT: Millbrook Press, Inc. Opposite approaches in known stories—*Goldilocks and the Three Bears* Two opposite approaches: 1. Turkle, B. (1976). *Deep in the Woods.* New York, NY: Dutton Children's Books. 2. Brett, J. (1990). *Goldilocks and the Three Bears.* New York, NY: Dover Publications.
Preschool and school age	Introduce cultural perspectives	Curious about other cultures; perhaps some prejudice about how other cultures live	Realistic books and stories about other cultures Kindersley, A., & Kindersley, B. (1995). *Children Just Like Me.* Bolton, ON: Fenn Publishing Company. Rattigan, J., & Hsu-Flanders, L. *Dumpling Soup.* (1993). New York, NY: Little, Brown and Company. Waters, K., & Slovenz-Low, M. (1990). *Lion Dancer Ernie Wan's Chinese New Year.* New York, NY: Scholastic Inc. Palazzo-Craig, J., & Nagano, M. (2001). *The Magic Peach: A Story from Japan.* Memphis, TN: Troll.

LISTING INCLUDES DIVERSITY IN RACE, GENDER, AND CULTURE

AGE	SKILL	BEHAVIOUR	EXAMPLES
Preschool and school age	Enjoy poetry Listening to rhyme, different forms of writing	Enjoy listening to poetry, rhyme Can recite simple to more complex poetry; rhyme with increased age (Photo A.42, p. 220)	Variety of poetry—nursery rhymes Moxley, S. (1995). *Skip Across the Ocean: Nursery Rhymes from Around the World.* London, UK: Frances Lincoln Ltd. De Coteau Orie, & Canyon, C. (1995). *Did You Hear Wind Sing Your Name? An Oneida Song of Spring.* New York, NY: Walker and Company. McConnell, R. (1978). *Norbert Nipkin.* Toronto, ON: Cerebrus Publishing Company Ltd.

Photo Gallery: Books and Reading

PHOTO A.37 Infants—look at books, identify pictures

PHOTO A.38 Toddlers—listen to and follow stories

PHOTO A.39 Toddlers and preschoolers—ask to have stories read

PHOTO A.40 Preschoolers—early reading; read and tell story using pictures and some words

PHOTO A.41 Preschoolers and school age—use books to look up information

PHOTO A.42 School age—increasing ability to read to others

TABLE A.6	Ages and Stages of Dramatic Play	
STAGE	**AGE**	**BEHAVIOURS**
Stage 1: Prop-dependent, imitative	1-year-olds	Imitate facial expressions and simple actions
	2-year-olds	Use props as intended, play directed by props (Photo A.43, p. 222)
		Solitary play
		Play parallel to others
		Imitate actions of peers or familiar adults
		Influenced by props—the prop will dictate the play
		Repeat actions or routines
		Use sound effects in their play
		Communicate through gestures, body language, and single words or phrases

STAGE	AGE	BEHAVIOURS
TABLE A.6 Ages and Stages of Dramatic Play *(continued)*		
Stage 2: Familiar roles	3-year-olds	Engage in role-play by taking on roles of significant adults in their lives (Photo A.44, p. 222)
		Interact with peers during role-play through actions and words
		May start to plan play by gathering props, and by identifying what they will do verbally
		Favourite themes include housekeeping, father and mother roles
		May have imaginary friends
		Dress-up
Stage 3: Diverse roles	4-year-olds	Take on roles of nonfamiliar adults (Photo A.45, p. 223)
		Take on adventurous roles, such as firefighter, police officer, pilot, construction worker
		State that this is a pretend activity
		Use a variety of items to represent props—symbolic representations
		Repeat favourite dramatic experiences
		Re-enact activities or events
		Increased time spent on dramatic activity
		Use variety of voice tones during play
Stage 4: Communicative, cooperative	5-year-olds and older	Create own characters
		Draw on characters from books and television
		Extensive discussions about play
		Increased attention to detail
		Start to use mime
		Extend play activity over more than one day (Photo A.46, p. 223)
		Involve several children
		Create own props
		Create own episodes in writing
		Create extensive plots

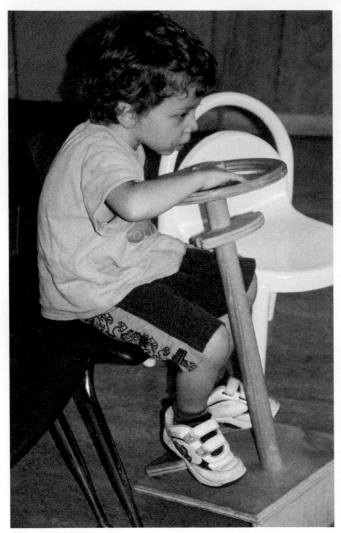

PHOTO A.43 One- and two-year-olds—stage 1, prop-dependent

PHOTO A.44 Two- to four-year-olds—stage 2, familiar roles

PHOTO A.45 Four-year-olds and up—stage 3, diverse roles

PHOTO A.46 Five-year-olds and up—stage 4, communicative and cooperative: build own dramatic play structures, characters, props

TABLE A.7	Stages of Artistic Development	
STAGE	**AGE**	**CHARACTERISTIC**
Stage 1: Scribbling: Beginnings of self-expression	2–4 years	Kinesthetic, manipulative, and expressive behaviours
Substage 1A: Disordered and random scribbling (Photo A.47, p. 225)	1½–2½ years	Large-muscle, whole-arm movement; kinesthetic pleasure Whole-hand grip May not look at paper while marking Haphazard lines May scribble beyond confines of paper Exploration—cause and effect—marks made when tools are moved across paper Lines made with single movement Tight grip with rigid wrist position Minimal finger movement

Table A.7 continues on next page

TABLE A.7   Stages of Artistic Development

STAGE	AGE	CHARACTERISTIC
Substage 1B: Controlled scribbling (Photo A.48, p. 226)	2–3 years	Smaller marks, better control Marking motions repeated Use wrist motion to gain more control Stay within confines of paper Variety of lines and directions appear Better visual and motor control of placement of lines Watch intently while scribbling More intricate loops and swirls appear Wider range of scribbles
Substage 1C: Named scribbling (Photo A.49, p. 226)	3½–4 years	Spend more time making markings Give names to scribbles, but name may change during process Relate scribbles to things in environment Hold marking tools with fingers, better fine motor control Greater variety of lines Increased concentration More intentional placement of marks Awareness of intentional use of empty space Appearance of scribbles may not match label given except to child artist Move from sheer physical expression to making marks that stand for something else by giving them a name
Stage 2: Preschematic (Photo A.50, p. 227)	4–7 years	Symbolic representation built up from other former scribbles that begin to be recognized by others Appearance of geometric forms Random placement and size and out of proportion Random floating spatial arrangement May turn or rotate paper while drawing Draw what they feel—leading to distortion and omission of parts of human figure drawing Head–feet presentation of human figure Over time, arms, body, fingers, toes, clothes, hair, and other details appear Objects drawn as isolated entities; no relationship Very personal idiosyncratic symbols Relative size appears at end of stage Learn that they can symbolically represent what they know or have experienced Colour used randomly Draw things important or relevant to self Objects are drawn facing forward

TABLE A.7	Stages of Artistic Development *(continued)*	
STAGE	**AGE**	**CHARACTERISTIC**
Stage 3: Schematic achievement of a concept (Photo A.51, p. 227)	7–9 years	Form concept is developed and repeated Drawings reflect children's concepts, not perception of an object Bold, direct flat representation Two-dimensional spatial representation Drawings reflect children's concepts, not perception of an object Baseline and skyline begin to appear Drawings reflect what children know Subjective portrayal of space X-ray drawings appear simultaneously, showing exterior and interior view Human figure made up of geometric shapes is repeated and refined Detailed and decorative Move to greater conformity or "stiffness" in drawing things the way they should be
Stage 4: Dawning Realism: The Gang Age (Photo A.52, p. 228)	9–12 years	Greater awareness of detail May be more self-conscious about their art Plane replaces baseline Objects drawn are smaller and less distorted

Adapted from Schirrmacher (2002).

Photo Gallery: Artistic Play

PHOTO A.47 1½ to 2½ years—scribble, substage 1A: disordered random scribbling

PHOTO A.48 Two to three years—scribble, substage 1B: controlled scribbling

PHOTO A.49 3½ to 4 years—scribble, substage 1C: named scribbling

PHOTO A.50 Four to seven years—stage 2, preschematic

PHOTO A.51 Seven to nine years—stage 3, schematic

PHOTO A.52 Nine to twelve years—stage 4, drawing realism

TABLE A.8	Ages and Stages of Math and Science Development	
AGE	**COMPONENT**	**POSSIBLE BEHAVIOURS**
Infants	Awareness Develop a general understanding/recognition of objects, people, events, concepts—provides basis for future learning (Photo A.53, p. 231)	Use senses to learn about shape, size, weight, and colour by looking at objects, touching, picking up, putting in mouth, dropping, manipulating Learn about space by being transported to different environments, placed in different environments; infants visiting siblings in child-care environments Learn about time—providing predictable routines—eating and sleeping based on infants' needs Learn about sequence—when I am wet, I feel wet. I cry, the caregiver comes, I get changed Mobile infants learn about more spatial terms—crawl under, crawl up or down Mobile infants start to make decisions—where to go, what to get, how to make things happen—throw, roll

AGE	COMPONENT	POSSIBLE BEHAVIOURS
Toddlers	Awareness—develop a general understanding/recognition of new objects, people, events, and concepts Develop more specific understanding/recognition of known objects, people, events, and concepts Exploration—sensory experiences to construct personal meaning about objects, people, events, and concepts (Photo A.54, p. 231)	Learn about weight and size by carrying, stacking, moving objects Learn about shape and colour by examining new objects, observing actions of others Learn about space by walking, running, climbing, riding, jumping Learn about time and sequence through regulated routines—eating, sleeping Stack objects, sort objects by colour, size, shape Match objects to pictures, label objects Develop sequence in play situations—wash baby, build and knock down towers, empty and fill Observe and imitate behaviours Discover relationships—cause and effect: When I push the ball, it rolls Create—drawings, paintings, structures
Preschoolers	Awareness—develop a general understanding/recognition of new objects, people, events, and concepts Develop more specific understanding/recognition of known objects, people, events, and concepts	Learn about concepts through manipulation, asking questions, looking at books, observing others Weight and size by carrying, constructing, manipulating Shape and colour by examining new objects, comparing objects, talking about objects Space by walking, running, climbing, riding Time and sequence through regulated routines—going to work, going to school, seasonal changes, dressing self, mealtime, nap time
Preschoolers	Explore—active experiences to construct personal meaning about objects, people, events, and concepts (Photo A.55, p. 232)	Match—find required objects in pictures, books Sort objects—colour, size, shape—easily distracted, may switch sorting criteria midstream (yellow bears to yellow cars to red cars) Measure—use rudimentary method (string, body) Compare—shells according to sound Match symbols to objects/pictures Develop sequence life cycles, seasonal Create own interpretations Discover relationships—seasonal changes Collect information—gather materials, make collections Count objects—may count incorrectly (missing numbers or repeating numbers); may not give correct answer when asked how many, even after counting One-to-one correspondence

Table A.8 continues on next page

TABLE A.8   Ages and Stages of Math and Science Development

AGE	COMPONENT	POSSIBLE BEHAVIOURS
Preschoolers	Inquiry—compare own results with others', look for similarities and differences	Examine items in different ways—by looking, using magnifying glasses, from different angles Investigate to see which item is heavier, which line is longer Give explanations based on personal perspective—jar is larger because it looks larger
	Utilization—apply understanding to new situations	Use past experiences that worked in new situations—used pitcher to pour water (easier to pour with spout); used pitcher to pour beads
School age	Awareness—develop a general understanding/ recognition of new objects, people, events, and concepts Develop more specific understanding/recognition of known objects, people, events, and concepts Explore—active experiences to construct personal meaning about objects, people, events, and concepts	Learn about concepts through writing, manipulation, asking questions, reading, performing operations and observing Weight and size by measuring with tape, scale, thermometer recording, calculating Shape and colour by examining new objects, comparing objects, talking about objects, representing objects Space by walking, running, climbing, riding, measuring, drawing, calculating Time—telling time, calculating time Classifying—objects, pictures, words Measure—use rudimentary method (string, body) Pattern—completes simple *abab* patterns, easily distracted to switch to new pattern (i.e., red car, blue car, red car, blue car, blue elephant, red car, yellow car, yellow elephant)
School age	Inquiry—compare their results with those of other sources, recognize commonalities and make generalizations	Compare—in writing, or representations Develop sequence—increased complexity Interpretations—on experiment/activity Discover relationships—between numbers, sets of numbers, among animals Collect information—gather materials, gather information in writing Count objects—count correctly, form sets of numbers Perform operations—addition, subtraction, division, multiplication, conduct simple experiments Explain results—verbally or in writing Compare results—with peers, in books Use conventional methods—formulas for solving problems, method for experimenting Generalize to new situations—create electric circuit, use to run Lego
School age	Utilization—apply understanding to new situations and settings (Photo A.56, p. 232)	Write reports, demonstrate principles, prepare presentations, discuss results, evaluate and re-adjust

Photo Gallery: Math and Science Development

PHOTO A.53 Infants—creating awareness of the world

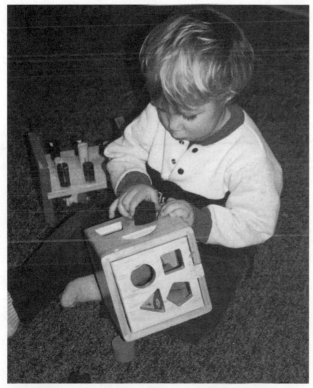

PHOTO A.54 Toddlers—develop understanding and recognition

PHOTO A.55 Preschoolers—explore to construct meaning

PHOTO A.56 School age—apply understanding to new situations

TABLE A.9 Ages and Stages of Woodworking

AGE	SKILL	MATERIALS
Infants–8 months and up	Push	Pop-up toys—push down on a button, a toy pops up or out
	Pull	Tops—push the button and the top spins
		Pull-apart toys—Duplo, ring-o-links
	Pound	Pounding toys—peg and hammer benches, ball maze (hammer ball into maze), pound coloured knobs to pop up toys
	Twist, turn	Turn keys on toy houses to open doors, dials on crib toys (Photo A.57, p. 234)
Toddlers	Play with wood pieces (sensory experience)	Wood of different sizes, shapes, weight (well sanded) to build with, paint, decorate
	Pounding toys	Hammers and pounding benches (Photo A.58, p. 234)
		Plastic or wooden workbenches—screws, screwdrivers, nuts, bolts, spanner
	Using tools—twist, turn	Take apart, build vehicles—screws, drills, nuts, bolts, screwdrivers, spanners
		Nuts and bolts sets
		Brio building set—use plastic tools and various shaped parts to construct creations
Three-year-olds	Hammer	Golf tees or large-headed nails into Styrofoam, fibreboard
		Nails into soft wood; nail two pieces of wood together (Photo A.59, p. 234)
	Screw	Insert screws into wooden board, screw in and out
	Attach	Various items to a piece of wood—with nails, glue
	Sand wood	Sanders (Photo A.60, p. 235)
	Decorate	Paint—rollers, brushes
	Saw	Thin pieces of soft wood clamped to workbench, child-sized saw
Four- and five-year-olds	Combine pieces to create an object	Saw wood to get correct size, measure pieces; use mitre box to cut angles; work on projects over time; attach pieces in various ways—glue, different-sized nails, screws (Photo A.61, p. 235)
		Use clamps to secure wood
	Follow a plan	Look up ideas for projects
	Use right-sized materials—nail to size to fit size of wood	
School age	Increasingly more skilled	Increasingly complex projects (Photo A.62, p. 236)

Photo Gallery: Math and Science Development

PHOTO A.57 Infants—push, pull, pound, twist, turn

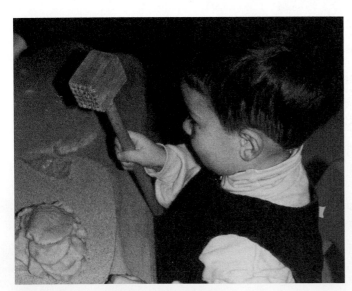

PHOTO A.58 Toddlers—pound, use tools

PHOTO A.59 Preschoolers (three-year-olds)—use tools

PHOTO A.60 Preschoolers—use tools

PHOTO A.61 Preschoolers (four- to five-years-olds)—combine pieces

PHOTO A.62 School age—plan and complete projects

REFERENCES

Crowther, I. (2003). *Creating effective learning environments.* Scarborough, ON: Nelson Thomson Learning.

Schirrmacher, R. (2002). *Art and creative development for young children.* Albany, NY: Delmar.

Theoretical Overview of Psychosocial and Cognitive Development: Erikson and Piaget

The psychosocial development stages defined by Erik Erikson (1902–1994) encompass the entire life cycle, recognizing the impact of society, history, and culture on personality. These stages of development are cumulative. At each stage of development, the individual must achieve certain tasks in order for positive development to occur. Failure to achieve these tasks may have long-lasting negative developmental results. Current research on brain development supports the philosophical underpinnings of this theory. Most early childhood programs in North America utilize Erikson's theory to explain psychosocial development.

The work of Jean Piaget (1896–1980) has long been used to explain children's cognitive development. Piaget defines the development in several cumulative stages, each of which describes the child's ability to solve problems and to understand the world. Although Piaget's theory has been criticized as underestimating cognitive development, it does present some evidence that children pass through a series of defined stages. Piaget's work provides a basis for discussion on cognitive development in most early childhood programs in North America.

Erikson's Stages of Psychosocial Development

STAGE	AGE	DESCRIPTION
I–Trust vs. mistrust	Birth–2 years	Infants learn to trust that their signals are understood and that the environment is a safe place to explore.
II–Autonomy vs. doubt	2–3 years	As toddlers gain increased skills and they are encouraged to actively explore their environment, they gain a sense of increased independence.
III–Initiative vs. guilt	3–5 years	The cumulative experiences of the first two stages and growth and development empower children to take the initiative. They learn to trust in their ability to act on their environment.
IV–Industry vs. inferiority	5–12 years	Children learn to become productive through increased attention and persistence and to take pride in their productivity.

Source: Adapted from Schickedanz, J., et al. (2001), and Berk, L. (2003).

Piaget's Stages of Cognitive Development

STAGE	AGE	DESCRIPTION
I–Sensorimotor	Birth–2 years	Infants actively explore the environment using their senses.
Reflexes	Birth–1 month	Infants' interactions are dominated by their reflexes.
Primary circular reactions	1–4 months	Infants develop control over their reactions. Reactions are a repeated action–stimulation–action sequence, usually involving touching, tasting, or making sounds.
Secondary circular reactions	4–8 months	Infants learn to control the things in their environment. When an infant shakes a rattle, it makes a sound. This action is pleasing, and so it is repeated.
Coordination of circular reactions	8–12 months	Infants' actions start to become intentional. The infant has a goal, such as picking up a toy and placing it into a container.
Tertiary circular reactions	12–18 months	Infants experiment to find different ways to accomplish the same thing.
Invention through mental combinations	18–24 months	Infants form mental representations (mental images) of objects and actions, and so they can learn to correctly place a geometric shape into a shape sorter. Learning is through trial and error.
II–Preoperational	2–7 years	Children interact with the objects and individuals in their environment through active play, based on personal perceptions. Interactions are egocentric—infants believe that everyone thinks and sees the world as they do. Children at this stage fail to understand concepts of space, quantity, causality, or time.
III–Concrete operational	7–13 years	The cumulative experiences of the previous stages and growth and development empower children to gradually understand such concepts as quantity, substance, length, area, mass, volume, space, and time through manipulation of real materials and real situations. Children begin to be able to interact with others and the materials in their environment through increased capability in abstract thought, such as reading, math, and writing.

Source: Adapted from Schickedanz, J., et al. (2001), and Berk, L. (2003).

REFERENCES

Berk, L. (2003). *Child development* (Cdn. ed.). Toronto, ON: Pearson Education Canada Inc.

Schickedanz, J., Schickedanz, D., Forsyth, P., and Forsyth, G. (2001). *Understanding children and adolescents* (4th ed.). Needham Heights, MA: Allyn & Bacon.

Glossary

acuity
sharpness of the visual image, or sound discrimination

apnea
prolonged periods when breathing stops

associative play
shares ideas and materials but continues to engage in solitary play

assertion of autonomy
infant starts to insist on independent action

babbling
stringing vowels and consonants together in strings of sounds (e.g., "ba-ba-ba-ba")

Babinski reflex
when sole of foot is stroked, toes fan and curl

binocular fixation
ability to focus on one object with both eyes

centration
focusing on only one aspect of a problem or situation

cephalocaudal
motor development progression from head downward to the legs and feet

competitive play
activities that have imposed rules and identify a winner or loser at the end of the play

constructive play
use of objects and materials to express ideas or create structures

contrast sensitivity
the degree of contrast that is needed in order for a pattern to be detected

cooing
strings of vowel sounds with different intonation patterns and of varying volume

cooperative play
two or more children work toward a common goal that includes sharing materials, ideas, and space, along with role designation

cruising
walking while holding on to furniture for support

decentration
ability to look at more than one aspect of a problem or situation at the same time

deferred imitation
spontaneously copying a behaviour or action seen previously

deictic gestures
gestures used to communicate the infant's intent

egocentric
sees the world only from own perspective, unable to understand another's

expressive language
verbal interaction or body language or gestures to initiate or respond to communication

eye–hand coordination
coordination of eye and hand movements to successfully pick up objects of varying sizes

fetal position
back curled, arms and feet close to body

fontanels
soft spots on the skull of an infant

functional play
repeated activity to practise existing or emergent skills

glial cells
cells that provide nutrients to the nerve cells, carry away waste products, and repair damage

holophrastic speech
one-word utterances that could be questions or statements, depending on the inflection used and accompanying gestures

joint attention
process in which two individuals focus on the same point of interest

lateralization
development of dominance in one or both cerebral hemispheres with regard to specific functions, such as speech, language, or creativity

Moro reflex
also known as the "startle response"; infant appears to be startled by an unexpected action or stimulant

myelination
process by which a protective sheath is formed around nerve fibres; this sheath helps to speed up the rate of impulse transmission

object permanence
infant searches for an object that is out of sight or hidden and therefore gains an understanding that the object continues to exist even when not seen

overextension
one word used to represent a broad category of items

palmar grasp
the hand and fingers move as one unit to pick up items

parallel play
play beside other infants using identical toys and in a similar type of play, but with no interaction

pincer grasp
using thumb and forefinger in opposition to pick up objects

pretend play
use of imitation and deferred imitation to act out roles and or situations

proto-words
word-like sounds accepted as real words

proximodistal
motor development progression from trunk outward to the arms and hands

receptive language
enables listener to understand what has been said

representational gestures
could symbolize an object, request, or characteristic

rooting reflex
when corner of mouth or cheek is stroked, infant turns toward source of stimulation

rote count
counting by memory without understanding the meaning of the numbers

scribble write
using scribbling with the intention of creating a written message

self-differentiation
process by which an individual gradually learns that he or she is a separate entity

separation anxiety
infant resists being separated from caregiver (cries, clings, refuses to let caregiver out of sight)

social referencing
infant looks to adult for approval of an activity or behaviour

solitary play
playing alone without interaction with others

stranger anxiety
infant clings to or hides behind caregiver or starts to cry when a stranger appears

sudden infant death syndrome (SIDS)
healthy infants die suddenly in their sleep for no apparent reason; danger peaks between 2 and 4 months, is over by 1 year of age

symbolic thought
using an action to represent a thought or idea

telegraphic speech
speech that resembles sentences but uses only the essential 2 to 3 words

temporal resolution
ability to differentiate between a light that is flashing and a light that is constant

tracking
visually following the movement of an object

trial-and-error learning
learning by trying different actions to get desired results

tripod grasp
using two fingers and the thumb to hold a writing tool

trundling
using alternate feet to propel a riding toy forward

turn-taking
listen and then respond appropriately

underextension
one word used to denote a particular thing when the word could actually be used to describe other items

visual accommodation
ability to change the shape of the eye's lens to focus on objects at different distances

Index